D1523877

The modern economic and social history of the Middle East in its world context

The political upheavals and momentous social and economic disturbances which the Middle East has witnessed during the last few decades will undoubtedly have a lasting impact on its people and the Muslim world in general. In this book the nature and effects of these changes are investigated by a distinguished body of social scientists specializing in the Middle East. Charles Issawi, the recipient of the Tenth Giorgio Della Vida Award in Islamic Studies, firstly puts recent historical trends into the context of the social and economic history of the Middle East as distinct from other world regions. Thereafter Roger Owen, Homa Katouzian, and Bent Hansen address the economic aspects of this history, paying close attention to past and current labor migration in the Middle East, oil and development since World War II, and economic development in Egypt around the turn of the century. Lastly, Samir Khalaf, Afaf Lutfi al-Sayyid-Marsot, and Carter Vaughn Findley focus on social change, emphasizing especially the relationship between traditional and modern loyalties, the changing role of women, and changes in education and the structure of knowledge. Together these essays offer a wealth of insight, theoretical argument, and information about salient aspects of Middle Eastern social and economic history.

Georges Sabagh is Director of the Gustave E. von Grunebaum Center for Near Eastern Studies and Professor of Sociology at the University of California, Los Angeles.

GIORGIO LEVI DELLA VIDA CONFERENCES

Gustave E. von Grunebaum Center for Near Eastern Studies, University of California, Los Angeles

TENTH CONFERENCE

The modern economic and social history of the Middle East in its world context

May 3–5, 1985

COMMITTEE

Reverend G. C. Anawati, O.P., *Dominican Institute, Cairo*
Amin Banani, *University of California, Los Angeles*
Richard G. Hovannisian, *University of California, Los Angeles*
Franz Rosenthal, *Yale University*
Georges Sabagh, *University of California, Los Angeles*
Bertold Spuler, *University of Hamburg*
Andreas Tietze, *University of Vienna*
Speros Vryonis, Jr., *New York University*
†Fazlur Rahman, *University of Chicago*
Recipient of the Ninth Giorgio Levi Della Vida Award in Islamic Studies

GIORGIO LEVI DELLA VIDA BIENNIAL CONFERENCE PROCEEDINGS

Issued under the auspices of the G. E. von Grunebaum Center for Near Eastern Studies, University of California, Los Angeles

1. Logic in Classical Islamic Culture, *edited by G. E. von Grunebaum (1970)*
2. Theology and Law in Islam, *edited by G. E. von Grunebaum (1971)*
3. Arabic Poetry: Theory and Development, *edited by G. E. von Grunebaum (1973)*
4. Islam and Cultural Change in the Middle Ages, *edited by Speros Vryonis, Jr. (1975)*
5. Individualism and Conformity in Classical Islam, *edited by Amin Banani and Speros Vryonis, Jr. (1977)*
6. Society and the Sexes in Medieval Islam, *edited by Afaf Lutfi al-Sayyid Marsot (1979)*
7. Islamic Studies: A Tradition and Its Problems, *edited by Malcolm H. Kerr (1980)*
8. Islam's Understanding of Itself, *edited by Richard G. Hovannisian and Speros Vryonis, Jr. (1983)*
9. Ethics in Islam, *edited by Richard G. Hovannisian (1985)*

GIORGIO LEVI DELLA VIDA CONFERENCES

Gustave E. von Grunebaum Center for Near Eastern Studies, University of California, Los Angeles

The Giorgio Levi Della Vida Medal of the Gustave E. von Grunebaum Center for Near Eastern Studies, University of California, Los Angeles, is awarded biennially to an outstanding scholar whose work has significantly and lastingly advanced the study of Islamic civilization. The scholar is selected by a committee appointed by the chancellor of the University of California, Los Angeles, meeting under the chairmanship of the director of the Gustave E. von Grunebaum Center for Near Eastern Studies.

The award carries with it a bronze medal and a prize of money, together with the obligation to present in person a formal lecture as part of a conference at the University of California, Los Angeles. The recipient of the award chooses the theme of the conference and selects the other participants. The proceedings of each conference are published in a special series, of which this volume is the tenth.

The first award was made in May 1967 to Professor Robert Brunschvig of the Sorbonne. Subsequent recipients have been Professors Joseph Schacht of Columbia University (1969), Francesco Gabrieli of the University of Rome (1971), Gustave E. von Grunebaum of the University of California, Los Angeles (1973, posthumously), Shlomo dov Goitein of Princeton University (1975), Franz Rosenthal of Yale University (1977), Albert Hourani of the University of Oxford (1979), W. Montgomery Watt of the University of Edinburgh (1981), Fazlur Rahman of the University of Chicago (1983), and Charles Issawi, of Princeton University (1985).

The editor would like to thank Marina Leasim Preussner, Principal Editor, von Grunebaum Center, for her invaluable help in the preparation of this volume.

Giorgio Levi Della Vida
1886–1967

The modern economic and social history of the Middle East in its world context

EDITED BY
GEORGES SABAGH

WITHDRAWN

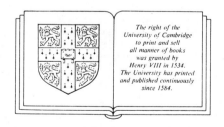

The right of the
University of Cambridge
to print and sell
all manner of books
was granted by
Henry VIII in 1534.
The University has printed
and published continuously
since 1584.

CAMBRIDGE UNIVERSITY PRESS

CAMBRIDGE

NEW YORK PORT CHESTER MELBOURNE SYDNEY

Published by the Press Syndicate of the University of Cambridge
The Pitt Building, Trumpington Street, Cambridge CB2 1RP
32 East 57th Street, New York, NY 10022, USA
10 Stamford Road, Oakleigh, Melbourne 3166, Australia

© Copyright 1989 by the Regents of the University of California

First published 1989

Printed in Great Britain by
Redwood Burn Limited, Trowbridge, Wiltshire

British Library cataloguing in publication data

Giorgio Levi Della Vida Biennial Conference (*10th:
1985: Gustave E. von Grunebaum Center for Near Eastern
Studies*).
The modern economic and social history of the Middle
East in its world context.—(Georgio Levi Della Vida
Conferences).
1. Middle East. Social conditions, history
I. Title   II. Sabagh, Georges   III. Gustave E. von
Grunebaum Center for Near Eastern Studies).
956

Library of Congress cataloguing in publication data

Giorgio Levi Della Vida Conference (10th: 1985: University of
California, Los Angeles)
The modern economic and social history of the Middle East in its
world context: [Tenth Giorgio Levi Della Vida Biennial Conference,
May 3–5, 1985. Gustave E. von Grunebaum Center for Near Eastern
Studies, University of California, Los Angeles] / edited by Georges Sabagh.
p.   cm.—(Giorgio Levi Della Vida conferences: 10th
conference)
Includes index.
1. Middle East—Economic conditions—Congresses.   2. Middle East—
—Social conditions—Congresses   3. Economic development—
—Congresses.   4. Social change—Congresses.   I. Sabagh, Georges.
II. Gustave E. von Grunebaum Center for Near Eastern Studies.
III. Title.   IV. Series.
HC415.15.G56   1985
330.956—dc19   89–725 CIP

ISBN 0 521 37351 4

RB

CONTENTS

Presentation of award to tenth recipient, Charles Issawi

GEORGES SABAGH

University of California, Los Angeles

During the last few decades the Middle East has witnessed political upheavals and momentous economic and social changes which will undoubtedly have a lasting impact on its people and on the Muslim world in general. A number of questions about the future of the Middle East should be answered in the light of these trends as well as those of a more distant past. What are the long-range consequences of the oil boom of the 1970s and the gap between "rich" and "poor" countries in the region? What are the implications of economic and technological dependency? Will the mass movement of people across Middle Eastern frontiers and between the Middle East and other world regions be sustained? What are the political, social, and economic effects of these mass movements? How and to what extent will women be incorporated in the processes of social, and economic change? What are the developmental assets and drawbacks of the Middle East, and how will they influence future economic development?

Answers to these questions require a full understanding of the economic and social history of the Middle East in comparison with other world regions. Who better than Professor Charles Issawi, who has devoted a lifetime to an analysis of this topic, to accomplish this task. In recognition of his unique and lasting contributions to the field he was selected as the recipient of the tenth Levi Della Vida award, at the first Levi Della Vida conference to focus on the economic facets of Middle Eastern and Islamic history. Previous conferences have dealt with social and ethical aspects of Middle Eastern history. While its more contemporary theme may seem to be a departure, the tenth Levi Della Vida conference shares with the preceding conferences their goal of a better understanding of the Middle East and of Islam through scholarly and insightful analyses.

Charles Issawi's sweeping view of the economic history of the Middle East is truly in the tradition of Gustave E. von Grunebaum, the founder and first director of the Center for Near Eastern Studies at the University of California, Los Angeles. Professor Issawi's many books and monographs on this topic include *The Economic History of the Middle East: 1800–1914* (1966), *The Economic History of Iran* (1971), *The Economic History of Turkey* (1980), *An Economic History of the Middle East and North Africa* (1982), and *The Fertile Crescent 1800–1914: A Documentary Economic History* (1988). Since 1975 Professor Issawi has been Bayard Dodge Professor of Near Eastern Studies at Princeton University. Prior to going to Princeton he was Ragnar Nurske Professor of Economics at Columbia University. His early experiences in the Egyptian Financial Ministry, as chief of research at the National Bank of Egypt, and as a member of the Middle East Economic Unit at the United Nations, have given him a unique insider's view of economic processes in the Middle East. All too often writings by economists conjure up highly abstract and humorless arguments supported by complex equations and extensive statistical data beyond the reach of many non-economists. Professor Issawi does not shun the use of statistics and theoretical arguments, but, as amply illustrated by his *Issawi's Laws of Social Motion* (1973), neither does he shun humor. His elegant and lucid prose reflects a humanist vision of the world.

The other participants in the conference were invited by Professor Issawi. Their contributions dovetail well with his essay and offer a wealth of insights, theoretical arguments, and information about various aspects of Middle Eastern economic and social history. Professors Roger Owen, Homa Katouzian, and Bent Hansen speak to the economic aspects of this history, paying particular attention to past and current labor migration in the Middle East, oil and development since World War II, and economic development in Egypt around the turn of the century. The chapters by Professors Samir Khalaf, Afaf Lutfi al-Sayyid-Marsot, and Carter Vaughn Findley focus on social change with a special emphasis on the relationship between traditional and modern loyalties, on changing women's roles, and on changes in education and the structure of knowledge. It is my hope that these chapters and the lead essay by Professor Issawi will inspire students of the social and economic history of the Middle East in the modern world to develop new and bold approaches to this history.

1 · The Middle East in the world context: a historical view

CHARLES ISSAWI
Princeton University

The Good Book says: "A prophet is not without honor, but in his own country" (Mark 6:4), and this great honor has been granted to me very far from my ancestral Syria, my native Egypt, or the East Coast where I have spent most of my life. It took nothing less than the grace of Nuestra Señora La Reina de Los Angeles to deem me worthy of such a distinction, and, as far as I am concerned, this has completely wiped out the resentment I felt as a New Yorker when your city stole the Brooklyn Dodgers. I am fully aware, however, that I do not measure up to the very eminent scholars who have preceded me. I can only believe that your intention was to show that the social sciences were worthy of inclusion in Islamic studies and, on their behalf, I thankfully accept your trust and have gathered for your benefit an excellent team of economists, economic historians, and social historians covering a wide spectrum of topics.

My starting point may be stated very simply. According to the economic and social criteria usually adopted in modernization studies (and which, with minor modifications, are also accepted by Marxists), during the last two centuries the Middle East has not – at least not until the very recent oil boom – done well compared to several other regions: Western Europe, Russia, the Balkans, Latin America, Japan, and China. This of course stands in sharp contrast with the brilliant earlier history of the Middle East. As regards economic criteria one can point to the following: the level of Gross National Product per capita and its rate of growth; the level of technology and its progress; the share of manufacturing in the GNP and its rate of increase; the distribution of income among various social classes; and a less quantifiable but nonetheless very important factor, the development of appropriate economic institutions.

As for social criteria one can mention the extremely high levels of

3

birth rates and rather high death rates, resulting in a very rapid rate of population growth; the low life expectancy; the low level of education, whether measured by mass literacy or by the proportion of children receiving secondary and higher education; and the depressed condition of women, as shown by their low rate of participation in the labor force, the much lower school attendance of girls compared to boys, and the restriction of certain fundamental legal rights, such as divorce. It is striking that in the various attempts made to measure social progress, such as the Physical Quality of Life Index, the Middle East stands much lower in the international scale than it does in the ranking of per capita incomes.[1]

My task in this paper will be to ask whether the long-term history of the Middle East can in any way reveal some factors that explain this relatively unsatisfactory performance. I will consider these factors with reference to the basic weaknesses, natural and social, in the Middle East and with regard to the nature and the effect of the European impact on the region. (I should also have discussed such external shocks as the Mongol invasion, the Black Death, and the diversion of trade around the Cape of Good Hope, but will not do so for lack of space.)

The world's earliest civilizations were born in the Middle East – in Iraq, Egypt, and Syria – which shows that given the technology and social structure of antiquity, the region's climate and natural endowments must have been favorable. Indeed, even in the early Middle Ages the Middle East, Muslim and Byzantine, was still one of the two main centers of the world economy, the other being China under the T'ang and Sung dynasties. This is indicated by all the accepted criteria: urbanization, literacy, the production of books, the state of crafts, the level and crop mix of agriculture, and the monetization of the economy. In all these areas the Middle East stood far ahead of all other parts of the world, with the exception of China. We all know about this brilliant period, and I shall not elaborate the point any further.

But what is most advantageous at stages A and B may not be so at stage C, and with the development of technology, the growth of population, the discovery and exploitation of new lands and resources, and the emergence of bigger social units, the relative advantages of other regions began to loom larger.

A major advantage was the abundance of navigable waterways, in contrast to the Middle East, which has only the Nile and the much less serviceable Tigris and Euphrates. One cannot overestimate the part played by rivers, especially when supplemented by canals, in the development of China, India, Russia, Europe, and North and South America. It is true that extensive use of camel and mule caravans made possible a large flow of goods overland; thus on the Tabriz–Trabzon route, in the 1870s, pack animals carried some 25,000 tons of merchandise a year, the equivalent of seven or eight shiploads each way. But of course the volume of goods carried by caravans was much smaller and the costs much higher than by waterways.

A closely connected factor is the lack of waterpower in the region. The water mill seems to have been invented in the Mediterranean[2] around the beginning of the Christian era, but for obvious reasons, it was used far less in the Middle East than in Europe. The role of the water mill in the economic development of Europe may be illustrated by three examples. First, "By 1086 William the Conqueror's Domesday Book records that the 3,000 settlements in England [whose total population was about 1,100,000] – most of them very small – averaged nearly two mills apiece."[3] This means that not only was there a much greater concentration of power than could be provided by men or animals (2 to 5 hp compared to 0.1 hp for a man, 0.66 hp for an ox and 2 hp for a camel), but also that machinery was brought into every village and its workings demonstrated for the whole population. Second, in the course of the next three centuries water mills were put to an unprecedented variety of uses in the textile, metallurgical, lumber, and other industries, and stimulated numerous inventions or borrowings, such as the cam and the crank. Lastly, as late as 1860, water mills provided 60% of the total horsepower in French industry, and only slightly less in the United States; high rates also prevailed in Britain, Switzerland, and elsewhere. It may also be noted that windmills, which seem to have been invented in Iran in the sixth century, played a very minor role in the Middle East but an important one in Europe, where they were greatly improved and were transformed into the most powerful engines the world had yet seen, up to 8 hp.

Another weakness connected with the aridity of the Middle East is the paucity of forests, except in Turkey and northern Iran. This was a heavy handicap since, until well into the nineteenth century, wood was everywhere not only the most important source of energy but also the basic industrial material. Not only were houses, ships, and bridges built of wood, but also the machines used in manufacturing and mining. Indeed, in the United States streets were often paved with wood.

In addition, the Middle East is rather poorly endowed with

minerals, except for oil, which assumed importance only in this century. Deposits of iron, copper, lead, gold, and silver are to be found in many countries, but they are almost always small. Coal is very scarce in the region, a fact whose importance may be gauged by considering that China has been burning coal since the fourth century and probably much earlier, and Western Europe since at least the thirteenth century.[4]

Last, and perhaps most important of all, is the fragility of the agricultural base in the Middle East. The larger part of the region has insufficient and very irregular rainfall, with violent annual fluctuations in production, the constant threat of droughts, and severe limits on expansion of cultivation; this applies to Iran, Iraq, Syria, and much of Anatolia. Irrigation provides a remedy, but its extent is strictly limited, and it usually requires elaborate and very vulnerable installations, such as the canals of Iraq and the *qanats* of Iran, which can be and often have been destroyed, with a consequent breakdown in the economy. The main exceptions in the Middle East are Egypt, with its splendidly regular and completely indestructible Nile, and the coastlands of Turkey.

The social factors may be considered under three headings: the alien nature of government; the inhibiting role of government; and the social composition of government.

It is a commonplace that, for nearly a thousand years, the rulers of the Middle East have been of foreign, usually Turkic, stock. It may well be that those Turks gave the region better government than its own indigenous peoples had provided. And it is certainly true that this phenomenon is not peculiar to the Middle East – one can think of the Turks and Moghuls in India, the Manchus in China, the Spaniards in Latin America, and others. Even England had its French-speaking Normans and Plantagenets, and it comes as a shock to read of the great English king, Edward I, "that he understood, and occasionally spoke, English is almost certain"[5] – his mother tongue being French, of course. But while many foreign dynasties eventually took over the culture of their subjects, in the Middle East most did not last long enough to do so. This is connected with another factor ultimately derived from the aridity of the region, namely, the presence on its fringes of large groups of pastoralists whose cohesion and mobility have enabled them periodically to sweep over large territories. Little need be said on this subject, since it has been admirably described and analyzed by Ibn Khaldun. In many ways, the Arab beduins may be included among the region's alien rulers. They too would eventually be civilized (or corrupted) by the bureaucracy and other institutions, but it usually took time and by then new nomads would come.

As regards the relation of government to society, a certain paradox may be observed. In late antiquity, while the Roman Empire broke down, the Byzantine and Sassanian empires survived, and their Arab conquerors soon succeeded in setting up a strong and fairly centralized government. And although the Arab empire soon broke up into many pieces the successor states remained quite strong. Hence, when in Western Europe the ground was cleared for the growth of numerous and vigorous independent centers of power and activity – Church, city states, feudal principalities, universities, guilds, and other associations – in the Middle East the continued power of the state discouraged such development. There were no independent city-states or universities; and guilds (whose existence before the Ottoman period has been questioned) were controlled by the government.

It is true that Middle Eastern governments refrained from interfering with many aspects of society, notably law, where Western governments, for instance, played the major role. But the inhibiting effect of the state in the spheres noted above deprived the region of those centers of independent activity which contributed significantly both to economic development and to the growth of political liberty in the West. Groups of producers – farmers, craftsmen, merchants, and others – did not have enough autonomy to establish associations and set up institutions that could further their interests and expand their economic base. And property was always insecure, as illustrated by the fact that so much trade and other economic activity passed into the hands of foreigners or minority members, who enjoyed foreign protection and therefore were safeguarded against the arbitrariness of officials.[6]

Closely connected with this is the third factor, the social composition of government. At least since the fall of the Fatimid Empire, the state apparatus remained in the hands of soldiers and bureaucrats, with some assistance from the ulama. Their main concerns were fiscal and provisioning: to raise enough taxes to meet their salaries and other expenses, such as war, regardless of the effect on production; and to ensure that the cities were adequately provided with foodstuffs, again regardless of the broader economic consequences or of the effects on the farmers. With much more justice one can apply to the Middle East David MacPherson's indictment of Europe, written in 1805, that no judicious commercial regulations could be drawn up by ecclesiastical or military men (the only classes who possessed any authority or influence), who despised trade and consequently could know nothing of it.

The economic consequences were disastrous. The Middle East had no counterpart to the monasteries, which played such an important role in promoting European agriculture, and the land tenure system meant that after the early Middle Ages there were no progressive landlords and that peasants had little or no incentive to improve their agricultural methods. The craftsmen were stuck in their old ways and the technical level of handicrafts may have actually declined; they certainly showed few signs of evolving into large manufactories, the way European ones did in the sixteenth and seventeenth centuries. In addition, the lack of concern by governments in the Middle East led them to conclude with European countries treaties that allowed goods to enter freely upon payment of minimal duties, usually 3% to 5%, and some industries began to suffer from this competition as early as the fourteenth century.[7] Since these treaties, and the Capitulations, were signed by the Mamluks and Ottomans at the height of their power, one must conclude either that those governments were uninterested in the economic consequences, or that they thought the damage done to the producers was a small price to pay for the benefits: larger imports of goods consumed by the ruling classes, or political objectives like alliances and support.

It is indeed striking to see how unconcerned Middle Eastern governments were with the broader objectives of commercial policy being pursued in Europe, like promoting exports to find markets for local products and to accumulate bullion, or restricting imports to protect local producers. No trace of Mercantilism can be detected in Ottoman or Iranian policy until well on in the eighteenth century, when certain minor measures were taken by Selim III.

Partly because the ruling groups looked down on mercantile activities, leaving many of them to the Christian and Jewish minorities, and partly because, in the eighteenth and nineteenth centuries, many members of these minorities managed to obtain foreign protection and to take advantage of the Capitulations, trade and shipping passed into their hands. This only increased the rulers' aversion to these and like occupations and made them further disinclined to give protection and encouragement to activities that could breed potentially hostile groups, as the Greeks had proved to be.

It should be added that the governments did nothing to promote transport, except for the building of a few bridges and caravanserais in a few cities and along some main routes. No roads were paved, no canals were dug, and no ports improved.[8] In fact, many harbors deteriorated because of neglect, as, for example, in Alexandria; silting, as in Jaffa and Suwaydia; or even deliberate blocking, as in Sidon and Beirut in the seventeenth century. By 1800 the Middle East was economically far behind its main rival, Europe, and, as will be shown, behind several other regions as well.

Social conditions were equally bad. No improvement in education had taken place since the Middle Ages; indeed, at the highest level there had been a sharp deterioration, as may be seen by comparing the curriculum of al-Azhar in 1800 with the sciences studied in the eleventh century. The literacy rate must have been well below 5%. The first census figures we have for any country, namely Egypt in 1897, are 10.5% for men and 0.3% for women overall, that is, including children but also the much more highly educated foreigners and minorities. Hygienic conditions were as bad as anywhere in the world, and the region was periodically swept by devastating epidemics of cholera and the plague.[9]

Perhaps most serious of all was the complacency and arrogance of the ruling classes and of the religious establishment, which made them look with indifference, and even contempt, on the tremendous intellectual changes that had taken place in Europe. It was only when European soldiers had penetrated the Balkans and invaded Egypt that they began to take notice.[10] It is worth recalling that, in 1485, Bayazit II prohibited printing in Arabic and Turkish, although in Istanbul books were being produced in Hebrew, Greek, and various European languages. The first Turkish press was opened in 1729, closed in 1742, and reopened in 1784. In 1610 a press printing psalms in Syriac was set up in the Lebanese monastery of Qazhayya, and in 1702 an Arabic press was set up in Aleppo; but the beginning of Arabic printing may more properly be dated from 1822, in Muhammad Ali's Cairo.[11]

Europe

To say that in the early modern period conditions in the Middle East were bad is not, however, very informative. My favorite definition of an economist is one who, when asked, "How is your wife?" replies, "Compared to what?" It is therefore necessary to compare the Middle East with other regions. One should start with Western Europe, since it was both the first region to modernize and the

Middle East's closest rival. I shall be brief, since I have discussed this subject elsewhere.[12]

I should begin by drawing your attention to an excellent recent book by E. L. Jones, *The European Miracle*.[13] In explaining Western Europe's lead Jones stresses the following factors. First, the natural environment is favorable: Europe is less exposed to geographical disasters (e.g., earthquakes and volcanic eruptions), to climatic disasters, (e.g., hurricanes, typhoons, droughts, etc.), to epidemics, locust invasions, and to human, crop, and animal diseases. Second, from a very early date, Europe had a pattern of dispersed settlement, nuclear families, and relatively late age at marriage; consequently less of its surplus was spent on the mere multiplication of life and more both on securing a relatively high level of living for its common people and on increasing its capital accumulation.

Three other sets of factors may be stressed: inventiveness; better economic practice and policy; and the great accretion of strength brought about by the discovery and colonization of the New World. Early medieval Europe far surpassed all other regions except China in its capacity to invent or borrow useful devices. Lynn White's superb study, mentioned earlier (cf. n.3 above), describes many such improvements. In agriculture there were the heavy wheeled ploughs, breast harnessing of horses, horseshoes, the common use of scythes, and the improvement of the harrow. The result was the development of the three-field system and the steady rise in grain yields, from levels far below those of the Middle East to far higher ones; at the same time Mediterranean Europe took over from the Middle East many tropical crops that had come there from Asia and Africa.[14] The use of water and windmills has already been mentioned. Shipbuilding improved steadily, and by the fifteenth century the Europeans were ready to launch their voyages of discovery. Armaments became more accurate and more deadly, giving Europe a decisive advantage in its encounters with other civilizations. Finally, starting with clocks and spectacles in the fourteenth century, Europe embarked on what may be called the high technology of the Middle Ages, and it has continued to lead the world until our times. In this context I should of course discuss the progress of European science, but this vast subject would take us too far afield. I should also mention the fact that by the late Middle Ages, western and southern Europe had a much higher rate of literacy than other parts of the world and that the lead widened steadily until the present century.[15]

As regards economics, Europe showed an early interest in numbers and the use of statistics. In the matter of economic practice we can point out such early developments as double-entry book-keeping and insurance. We can also observe that European economic structures, like the political ones, were larger, more complex, and more durable than those of other cultures. Among many examples may be cited medieval guilds, banks, maritime convoys, and such institutions as the Hanseatic League. The contrast between the latter and its Middle East counterpart, the Karimis, is instructive; the Karimis' volume of trade may have been even larger, but their overall position was weaker and they proved far more ephemeral.

Lastly, there is economic policy. Medieval European governments, like Middle Eastern ones until much later, were very much concerned with provisioning and the avoidance of famine. But in most city-states, to quote Cipolla, "There was a conscious effort to industrialize. At the beginning of the fourteenth century the conviction was widespread that industry spelled welfare. In a Tuscan statute of 1336, statements may be read which might have been written by the most modern upholders of industrialization in the twentieth century."[16] Such national monarchies as England and France also took industrial and commercial needs into account, adopting appropriate measures to foster industries; they sought to increase exports with a large "value added" component and restrict imports of competitive goods, while encouraging imports that served as inputs into goods supplying important local needs or designed for export. Another manifestation of the same policy is the enactment of the Navigation Laws to stimulate local shipping; such laws were passed as early as the thirteenth century. The energetic measures taken to stabilize European currencies after the great inflation of the sixteenth century stand in striking contrast to the policy of the Ottomans and Safavids, and European taxes were somewhat more rational and less oppressive. Perhaps most important, property was far more secure in Europe than anywhere else in the world. The principal reason was probably the fact that producers – landlords, merchants, craftsmen, and industrialists – were more fully represented in government and had more influence on its policy than in other regions, and this in turn may be traced to the collapse of the Roman Empire and the consequent emergence of independent centers of activity mentioned earlier.

Japan

I shall also deal briefly with Japan, since I have discussed it too elsewhere at some length.[17] Perhaps the simplest way to point out the contrast between Japan and the Middle East is to say that early in the nineteenth century, well before it had been "opened up," Japan was a highly modernized country in every respect except technology. This may be studied with three headings: political, social, and economic.

Among the favorable political factors may be mentioned Japan's almost unparalleled ethnic, linguistic, and religious homogeneity, which has spared it many of the travails afflicting other societies. This homogeneity is reinforced by the extraordinary cohesion shown by the Japanese in both war and peace, and their readiness to subordinate their individual interests to those of a larger group, be they the state's or Toyota's. Japan achieved unity very early – by the seventh or eighth century – and by and large has succeeded in maintaining it. The central government exercised a fair measure of control over the land, enough to ensure peace and to carry out the few major public works that were deemed necessary. Village solidarity was also strong and much authority could be left to local bodies without endangering stability. After its unsuccessful invasion of Korea and its defeat by the Chinese at the Yalu river in 1593, Japan withdrew into itself and had three centuries of peace. Lastly, Japan produced a ruling class which eventually carried out what is perhaps the most spectacular modernization in history. Moreover, it was a ruling class that was willing to learn from others.

In 1868, Prince Iwakura Tomomi led an amazing mission abroad. A large number of the most senior Japanese government leaders left their posts temporarily and visited the United States and Europe from 1871 to 1873 to learn about Western technology, government, business and society. They applied their newfound knowledge throughout the Japanese economy.[18]

The social record is even more impressive. For some 150 years Japan managed to keep its population constant at about 30 million, partly because of the usual Malthusian checks but also because of deliberate control by means of abortion and infanticide. Birth rates were distinctly below those of most other regions, including the Middle East, and so were death rates; more generally, health conditions seem to have been relatively good. Urbanization was extraordinarily high. By 1720, Tokyo had about 1 million inhabitants, matched only by London and Peking; Osaka and Kyoto had about

400,00 each; and some 12% of the total population lived in towns of 10,000 or more inhabitants, a figure higher than that for all but three or four European countries. Education was widespread, and by the 1850s "an estimated 40 per cent of the male population and 10 per cent of the female had achieved some degree of literacy." In the cities the figures were much higher, being put at 75% to 85% for males. One result was a very large publishing industry; in the 1780s some 3,000 titles were being published each year, editions of more than 10,000 were not uncommon, books were cheap, and both free and commercial lending libraries were active – conditions that compare favorably with the most advanced European countries.[19] Lastly, there was a keen intellectual curiosity and willingness to learn from other cultures, first China, then Europe. In the late seventeenth century some Japanese started learning Dutch, and in the eighteenth they began systematically to study Western technology, science, and painting; soon a small number of Japanese had become familiar with Newtonian physics and Western physiology.[20]

As regards the economy, perhaps the most striking aspect was the effort, sustained over several centuries, to raise agricultural output by using better methods, selecting seeds, experimenting with various types of organic fertilizers, introducing new cash crops, and so forth. An eighteenth-century book on sericulture had a first printing of 3,000 copies, and many books on agriculture went through several editions. As a result, Japanese yields were among the very highest in the world, and rose steadily.

Japanese handicrafts were at a very high level and were widespread in the villages as well as the cities. Because of Japan's isolation, these crafts were exposed to European competition far later than those of the Middle East, India, Latin America, or even China, and survived longer, to play an important part in the country's industrialization, particularly in the textile and ceramic industries but also in many other branches, through subcontracting. They also survived longer because of the peculiar pattern of Japanese development: the Japanese soon picked up European production methods but retained their traditional consumption patterns until very recently, whereas the people of the Middle East (and others) soon learned to consume *alla franga* but are only just beginning to adopt Western production methods. In the last few decades the pattern of consumption of the Japanese has changed, but their strong preference for homemade goods has persisted, to the chagrin of American and European exporters; in this area too the contrast with the Middle East is very marked.

Other economic matters that may be mentioned are the high degree of monetization and the well-developed credit institutions and instruments including paper money, checks, and even "future transactions in rice" in Osaka in 1730. Double-entry bookkeeping, some of it on a very high level, was practiced, and what was possibly the world's first department store was established by the Mitsui family in Tokyo in 1683. Perhaps most striking is the prevailing work and profit ethic, attested in the large number of commercial, agricultural, and other books used in Japanese schools.[21] It should also be added that Japan had natural resources adequate for the preindustrial and early industrial period, including iron, copper, coal, wood, and water power, and that its navigable rivers and long coastlines greatly facilitated transport.

Russia

A comparison of Russia with the Middle East at the beginning of the nineteenth century would, at first sight, reveal little difference. Grain yields were somewhat lower in Russia,[22] the products of the handicrafts were inferior, urbanization was far lower, literacy little if at all higher, and transport costs distinctly higher. The main factors that had held up Russia's development for so long – isolation from Western Europe, the burden of an unhappy history, the huge distances and harsh climate which made it so difficult to exploit the country's vast riches, and the vicious institution of serfdom – still held the country in their grip. A closer look, however, reveals other factors at work which over the next hundred years were to produce a vast difference between the two regions.

First of all, Russia had a strong government. The armies that had defeated Charles XII and raided the neighborhood of Stockholm, overpowered Frederick II and occupied Berlin, and chased Napoleon all the way to Paris, and the navy that, sailing from the Baltic, had captured Beirut in 1772, presuppose an efficient bureaucracy, a good organization providing munitions and supplies, and a great capacity to raise taxes. During Peter's reign tax collections increased fivefold, and they went on increasing under his successors. Moreover, the government was keenly aware of the need for economic and social development and had been taking many measures to bring this about. As early as 1569 some English industrialists were encouraged to build ironworks in Russia, and in the course of the next hundred years many enterprises in metallurgy, glass, sugar, and other branches were set up by foreigners. In

1652 a special quarter, the *sloboda*, was established in Moscow for foreign craftsmen.[23] Peter made much greater use of the foreigners than his predecessors had, but he went further, implementing a mercantilist policy for developing the economy. Canals were dug, shipyards were built, and many industrial enterprises were undertaken. But, like his European contemporaries, Peter believed that the bulk of development would have to be carried out by private enterprise, and he set out to "manufacture the manufacturers," protecting them with high tariffs and other measures and encouraging them with loans and various privileges. In 1718 three colleges or boards (for business, manufactures, and mines) were created to oversee development and grant privileges to those qualified.[24]

Peter's successors continued to encourage industry and mining but gave private enterprise rather more scope.[25] As a result, the number of factories multiplied many times over and their average size increased. Russia's iron industry became, for some decades, the biggest in the world, and there was a large expansion in textiles, sugar, and some branches of the chemical industry.[26] A small number of entrepreneurs, mostly former merchants but some ex-serfs, also came to control large industrial enterprises in the Urals, Moscow, and elsewhere. This economic expansion was accompanied by a good deal of inventiveness. A list of Russian innovations in applied science and industry in the late eighteenth and early nineteenth centuries makes impressive reading, even after discounting for the Soviet tendency to claim Russian firsts in every field, from the invention of the wheel to the marvels of the twenty-first century.[27]

There was also much intellectual progress. The first printing press was established in 1553, although output remained small. Peter's approach to education was strictly practical: he opened engineering, naval, artillery, and mathematical schools, and founded a newspaper in 1703 called *News of Military and Other Affairs Worthy of Knowledge and Memory*; he founded the Academy of Sciences, opened just after his death in 1725. He forced the nobility to send their sons to government schools. Moscow University was founded in 1755 and was followed by four gymnasia. At the very beginning of the nineteenth century two more universities were established (at Kazan and St. Petersburg) and forty gymnasia.[28] Thus a base was laid for Russia's tremendous intellectual advance in the nineteenth century.

It is interesting to follow developments in the field of social thought. Even before Peter several economists had shown a good

understanding of the situation in Russia, notably Ordin-Nashchokin (1605–80) and Pososhkov (1652–1726); in 1720, the latter wrote
the important *Book on Poverty and Wealth*. In 1738 the first manual
on agricultural economics was published. The encyclopaedic mind
of Lomonosov (1711–65) addressed historical and linguistic questions as well as those of natural science. In 1765 the Free Economic
Society was established, and between 1787 and 1792 the *Commercial Dictionary*, the first economic encyclopaedia in Russia, was
published.[29] It is worth noting that the Russian translation of Adam
Smith's *Wealth of Nations* appeared in 1802–6, only twenty-six years
after the English edition. Under Catherine, Nikolai Novikov (1744–
1818) wrote some very incisive criticisms of Russian society, and his
book enterprises published some 900 titles, while Alexander Rad-
ishchev (1749–1802) wrote his famous *Journey from St. Petersburg
to Moscow*.[30] Let me just add that in 1820 the Imperial Library in St.
Petersburg had 300,000 volumes, a figure exceeded only by the
Royal Library in Paris, the Bodleian at Oxford, and the Archival
Library in Munich.[31]

In other words, the heavy Russian dough was being leavened by
both economic and intellectual progress. The results were soon to
be visible, on the one hand, in Russia's cultural florescence, and on
the other, in the industrial upsurge of the 1830s to 1850s.[32] The
abolition of serfdom in 1861 made possible a swift capitalist development that registered the highest rate of industrial growth in
the world, laid the world's second largest network of railways,
began to improve land tenure and agricultural methods, spread
education so that the literacy rate among recruits rose from 30% in
1888 to 68% in 1913,[33] and, but for the shattering effects of World
War I, might well have carried Russia to some form of consti-
tutional bourgeois government.

The Balkans

A few words may be said about the Balkans. Today, by any economic or social criteria, the region is far ahead of the Middle East.
Before World War I it was well ahead in the social field and in
certain economic aspects, for example, industrialization and railway mileage, but not in others, such as per capita income or foreign
trade. And yet around 1800 the Balkans were in most respects no
better off than most of the Middle East. Grain yields may have been
slightly higher.[34] Transport was probably no better: more carts were
used and more rivers were navigable, but the terrain was muddier

and rougher and camel transport was not available. In some areas, notably Bulgaria, handicrafts were more widespread, but the region lacked the high crafts of Istanbul, Cairo, Aleppo, and Isfahan.[35] Literacy was probably slightly, though surely not much higher, but urbanization was far lower: the largest town, Salonika, had less than 70,000 inhabitants and remained in Ottoman hands until 1912.

The Balkans have one important natural advantage over the Middle East: higher and more regular rainfall, resulting in more forests, more water power, and more navigable rivers. But the secret of the area's better performance lies more in the political and social fields. First of all, the Balkans obtained independence much earlier and, although Balkan governments were far from being models of stability or enlightenment, they were more responsive to their national needs. They helped the economy by giving protection, building infrastructure, and extending credit, and by bringing about some industrialization before World War I. Second, and more important, Balkan societies were far healthier than those of the Middle East. This may be observed in many aspects.

First and foremost, an enormous majority of peasants came to own their land, and since for a long time population density was light their plots were adequate. In Serbia, "old" Greece and Thessaly, and Bulgaria, land distribution came about with independence and the departure of the Turkish ruling class, and in Croatia with the Austrian reforms of 1848. Only Roumania had a large – and parasitic – landlord class and a very deprived peasantry, in spite of the agrarian reform law of 1864 and other measures taken by the Roumanian government.[36] As a result, many foreign travellers commented favorably on living standards and the prevalent social equality.[37] Another result of this equality, and of the development of cash crops for export to central and Western Europe,[38] was the growth of rural cooperatives, which both met some of the farmers' credit needs and helped them improve production.[39]

Second, the Balkan population was distinctly more educated than the Middle Eastern. Already in the seventeenth and eighteenth centuries students were sent to Europe, books in the various vernaculars were printed in Europe and sent to the Balkans, and many schools were established in Greece.[40] Trade with Austria and Italy also opened channels for new ideas, and Ragusa (now Dubrovnik) was a powerful center of Enlightenment. After independence many schools were opened, general, monitorial and technical. By 1910, some 35% to 40% of children aged 5 to 14 were attending primary school, and secondary enrollments were also high; moreover, a large proportion of those in secondary and higher education were engaged in technical training.[41] By 1907 Greece had achieved a literacy rate of 39% and Bulgaria of 34%, compared to Egypt's 7%, and even lower figures for the rest of the Middle East; by 1927 the figures were 60% for Bulgaria and Greece compared to 15% for Egypt and 8% for Turkey.[42] Third, birthrates began to decline shortly before World War I, and by the 1920s and 30s had fallen to low levels.[43]

Lastly, the Balkan countries profited from the emigration of hundreds of thousands of their citizens to the New World, Russia, Egypt, and elsewhere. Money was remitted, skills were acquired, and new ideas were brought back. Of all the Middle Eastern countries only Lebanon enjoyed this stimulus, though mention may be made of the Iranians in the Caucasus.

A few words are necessary on Greece. The most disadvantaged country in terms of resources, its inhabitants have always engaged in trade and shipping. Already by the eighteenth century Greeks accounted for a very large proportion of Ottoman trade and shipping as well as of southern Russian. Greeks were also extensively employed in the Ottoman bureaucracy. A Greek bourgeoisie came into being early and played an important role in the political, cultural, and economic development of both Greece and its neighbors.

Latin America

Latin America is too complex an area to discuss here, but I should like to say a few words about two countries, Argentina and Mexico, which may be taken to represent, respectively, the empty, temperate, and fertile southern region, and the densely settled area of ancient civilizations in the north.

In the eighteenth century, Buenos Aires grew into a town of more than 50,000 as a port of entry for the great silver-mining center of Potosi, in present-day Bolivia. After independence Buenos Aires developed into an export center for hides, wool, and other animal products, and after 1860 began to attract large amounts of capital and immigrants, enabling Argentina to lay down 35,000 kilometers of railways by 1914 and to become a major exporter of wheat and meat. By 1914 Buenos Aires had 1.5 million inhabitants and real wages there were some 25% higher than in Paris. Large-scale industrialization began in the 1880s and continued at a rapid rate until the end of World War II. The growth of GNP was such that

Argentina compared favorably with Australia and Canada, and its culture was almost on a European level. All this, *dependencia* theory notwithstanding, presents no problem for the old-fashioned economic historian who believes in development based on the export of a staple product.[44] The real mystery is why Argentina has performed so poorly since the last war, and my suspicion is that politics in general, and Juan Peron in particular, have much to answer for; however, the effect of falling export prices should not be underestimated.

Mexico did not have Argentina's assets – immensely fertile land, abundant and regular rainfall, and navigable rivers – and its history has been much more checkered, starting with the shrinkage of the Indian population from perhaps 20 million in 1500 to 1 million in 1600.[45] But what should be stressed is that around 1800, Mexico (along with most of Latin America) was a richer and much better educated place than the Middle East.

As regards wealth, in the eighteenth century Mexico experienced a great upsurge in both population and production, including mining, agriculture, and handicraft industry.[46] Available figures suggest that per capita GNP in Mexico was from a third to a half that in the United States – and it may be noted that Mexico accounted for about one-half of the total population and product of Spanish America.[47] Mining technology was quite advanced and improved steadily, the handicrafts were active, the big estates received much capital investment, and trade, both legal and contraband, was very large; there were many substantial merchants (some with a capital approaching $500,000) who gave and took extensive credit.[48]

All this does not of course mean that the level of living of the masses was high. First, there was the enormous unrequited drain of silver to Spain: for 1785 the total for the colonies has been put at $30 million, compared to $6.5 million for India in the same year.[49] Second, there was the vast inequality due to ethnic composition and social stratification. At the end of the eighteenth century one-fifth of Mexico's population was Spanish and another fifth of mixed race; three-fifths were Indian, a figure comparable to that for a few parts of Spanish America, but much higher than for others.[50] At the top were some estates worth $2 to $3 million.[51]

This wealth made it possible to support an impressive educational establishment. Printing presses were set up at the Conquest, as early as the 1550s universities were opened in Lima and Mexico City and by the end of the colonial period there were more than twenty institutions of higher learning, including a College of Mines opened in Mexico in 1792; among them they had conferred 150,000 degrees.[52] They were modeled on Salamanca, then one of the largest (7,000 students) and most active universities in Europe.[53] In addition many students went abroad, not only to Spain but to France, Italy, and England.[54] And of course Spain was always part of the European cultural stream, even if it was somewhat of a backwater. As a result, Latin Americans participated very fully in the Enlightenment – in philosophy, physics, mathematics, and biology – and were familiar with (and often critical of) the works of Descartes, Newton, Locke, Leibnitz, Adam Smith, Buffon, Franklin, and others. This is brought out very clearly by a study based on the theses written by students at the rather small University of San Carlos in Guatemala.[55] In addition, intellectuals applied themselves to local problems, ranging from botany and medicine to economics.[56]

Clearly, Latin America was well ahead of the Middle East in 1800. The great destruction and anarchy following independence, however, set the region back. To take two examples, it was only around 1880 that the 1810 level of silver output was regained; and the University of Mexico was closed repeatedly between 1833 and 1865, and finally shut down in the latter year. The region had to start its upward climb painfully again in the last decades of the nineteenth century.

China

I do not have the presumption to survey the history of China, but I would like to point out that, until the eighteenth century, it was always at the forefront of economic, technological, and even scientific progress. It had also produced a highly educated society. Printing had been practiced on a large scale since the seventh century, and in the eighteenth and nineteenth centuries "perhaps 30 to 45 percent of the males and only 2 to 10 percent of the females [possessed] some ability to read and write."[57] Following a series of shattering internal and external shocks in the first half of the nineteenth century, the society broke down and China experienced nearly a century and a half of intense disruption. It now seems set to become once again one of the most dynamic societies in the world.

I hope that by now, the point I have been trying to make is clear: the Middle East entered the nineteenth century at a disadvantage, economically and socially, compared to the other regions surveyed.

We still need to ask, however, why the Middle East did not catch up in the next two centuries. The reasons are to be sought in two sets of external and internal factors.

Impact of Europe

As regards the external, the Middle East was subjected to a very powerful European impact in the political, economic, and social spheres.[58] This had many beneficial results. Foreign trade multiplied many times over, agricultural output expanded greatly, new crops were introduced, railways and ports were built, hygiene improved noticeably, and the foundations of modern education were laid down. The region began to modernize at an accelerating pace. But in addition to the usual painful disruptions accompanying any change, there were several adverse developments – though nothing, I should hasten to add, comparable to the earlier drain of bullion from Latin American and India, the export of slaves from Africa, and the Opium War and its aftermath in China. First of all, as in all parts of the world, improved hygiene and mechanical transport, which reduced famines, led to population growth, through a drop in the death rate; in the Middle East, however, the birth rate started declining much later than elsewhere, and in fact in many countries it still shows no signs of decrease. The result has been an explosive population growth that has put great strain on resources. Second, again as in all parts of the world, the handicrafts suffered from the competition of machine-made goods, and many were ruined; however, reindustrialization – the setting up of modern factories – started later in the Middle East, and was much slower there than in Russia, the Balkans, Latin America, Japan, India, and in many respects, China. This was partly due to the smallness of internal markets and the paucity of natural resources, infrastructure, capital, and skills; partly to the baleful effects of the Commerical Treaties, which prevented tariff protection; and partly to the lack of interest of governments, whether national (with the conspicuous exception of Muhammad Ali) or foreign. It was only in the 1930s, and more particularly after the World War II that the region began to industrialize.

Third, there was the huge volume of public debt, most of which was squandered. Again, the Middle East is not unique in this respect, the record of the Balkans and Latin America being equally poor (but not that of Russia, India, and Japan). Whether the Middle East was treated more harshly than other regions in its terms of settlement is moot: Egypt probably was, but Turkey was not. The large amount of private capital that flowed in was, on the whole, used productively.

Fourth, to a particularly high degree, economic development in the Middle East was implanted by foreigners and remained confined to an enclave. The region not only took capital and technology from abroad; it imported a bourgeoisie and a skilled working class as well. Except for members of the religious minorities, few Middle Easterners participated in the expanding modern sectors of the economy – foreign trade, finance, mechanical transport, mining, and later industry – which were financed and run by Europeans. As a result, the natural resources of the Middle East were developed, but not the human resources. Moreover, in contrast to Russia, the Balkans, and Latin America, foreigners did not eventually blend with the population through intermarriage and permanent residence. And it was only in the 1930s and 1940s that a national Muslim bourgeoisie emerged.

I should perhaps add one more point. Because of its political situation, the Middle East in some ways had the worst of both worlds. Unlike Japan, Russia, the Balkans, and Latin America, the countries of the Middle East did not enjoy independence, with the chance to make and also learn from mistakes. Nor were they subjected to the kind of control that led to much development by the British in India, the Russians in Azerbaijan, the Japanese in Taiwan, or the Americans in the Philippines. Instead, most often, there was the influence of rival powers jealously watching and checking each other, preventing railway building in the Ottoman Empire and Iran and thwarting other schemes. Of course, the experience of North Africa shows that direct foreign control, too, can lead to much development of resources with very little benefit to the indigenous population.

To these external factors must be added an internal one, which is best described as a lack of sustained interest in economic development. It is true that the governments were greatly handicapped by the Capitulations, Commercial Conventions, foreign pressures, and lack of funds; but it cannot be seriously argued that they could not have done more to promote the economy and especially education. Even more striking is the indifference of the people themselves. After all, it does not take much money to teach children – or adults – how to read and write, but it does take work. One should note that in Western Europe, Japan, and elsewhere the raising of literacy rates to the first crucial 40% or 50% was achieved not by the state but by churches and other social agencies. Here one can contrast the very limited efforts made by the ethnic Turks, Arabs, and Iranians not only with those of their Balkan neighbors and others but also with those of their minorities – Greeks, Armenians, Jews, and Christian Arabs. The minorities were economically much more successful, a fact partly due to foreign help and protection but also to the numerous schools they set up and their pursuit of technical and professional education.[59] One more point may be briefly made. The vast majority of Middle Easterners who went to study abroad did not go in for science, economics or, except for a small number of engineers, technology. Most of them studied law, and a few studied medicine and letters. This too must have had an adverse effect on economic development.

In the last fifty years or so this dismal picture has changed markedly. Industrialization has spread rapidly and has been greatly strengthened by the development of oil, which has generated vast income and skills and provided raw materials and fuels. The infrastructure has been vastly expanded and is now approaching adequacy. Land reforms have transformed the ancient, vicious agrarian structure. The economy has been wrested from foreign hands and is now run by nationals.

Hygiene has considerably improved and life expectancy has doubled to sixty years. The region is beginning to draw on the enormous resources, hitherto almost unused, of half its population as women participate much more actively in economic and social activity. Perhaps most encouraging of all is the progress in education, best indicated by the fact that adult literacy, which just after World War II averaged about 20%, has risen to 50% or more. At the higher level, the region now has tens of thousands of men and women trained in science, technology, economics, and statistics, some of whom are doing excellent work. The progress in education can be traced, chronologically and comparatively, in the illuminating tables compiled by Richard Easterlin, showing school enrolment rates per 10,000 inhabitants.[60] If we take a figure of 1,000 as indicating the level of primary education that allows a country to absorb technology and therefore embark on rapid economic development, we can see that the three major Middle Eastern countries – Egypt, Iran, and Turkey – reached that level by 1960; as late as 1930 the figure was only 300 for Turkey, less for Egypt, and far less for Iran. By contrast, Western Europe had reached it by the first half of the nineteenth century, the United States still earlier, Japan and Russia at the turn of the century, and the larger Latin American countries in the 1920s or 30s.

Of course the Middle East is still beset by tremendous problems:

explosive population growth, urban hypertrophy, lagging agricultural production, the stifling grip of the government over the economy. And it is truly sad to see the waste of resources on unending wars and ever-accumulating armaments. But it is not excessively optimistic to state that the foundations of economic and social development have at last been laid.

I should like to conclude with one more observation. Hitherto, my analysis of the region's economic and social performance has been confined to physical and social factors. I should like to make a brief excursion into the treacherous realm of mentality. Oversimplifying and generalizing wildly, one can say that whereas the Greeks were interested in ideas, the Romans in organization, the Chinese and Japanese in things and organization, and the Europeans in ideas and things, the Middle Easterners have been interested in words, but also in God; and, as a Middle Easterner reminded us, "The Word was God." The latter interests do not tend to promote economic and social development. But consider what they have enabled the region to achieve: the Sumerians and Egyptians started the whole process of civilization; the Phoenicians invented the alphabet and initiated the mercantile city-state economy which, as Hicks points out, was the most important economic development since the establishment of agriculture.[61] The Jews, Persians, and Arabs between them gave most of the world's great religions. Add to this some of the finest art and literature. These contributions surely outweigh a certain deficiency in the technological, economic, and social fields, especially since there is nothing that decrees that the region will not do better in those fields in the future than it has in the past. Furthermore, we do live in a time when many have come to realize that economic growth and technological development are not the most important things in the world.

NOTES

1 Roger Hansen and Valeriane Kallab, eds., *United States Foreign Policy and the Third World* (New York: Praeger, 1982), pp. 155–9.
2 K. D. White, *Greek and Roman Technology* (London: Thames & Hudson, 1984), pp. 55–6.
3 Lynn White, *Medieval Technology and Social Change* (Oxford: Clarendon Press, 1962), p. 155.
4 E. Reischauer and J. Fairbank, *East Asia, The Great Tradition* (Boston: Houghton Mifflin, 1960), p. 178; *The Cambridge Economic History of Europe*, Vol. II (Cambridge: Cambridge University Press, 1952), pp. 125, 160, and 434.

5 L. Salzman, *Edward I* (London: Constable, 1968), p. 190.
6 See Charles Issawi, "The Transformation of the Economic Position of the *Millets* in the Nineteenth Century," in Benjamin Braude and Bernard Lewis, eds., *Christians and Jews in the Ottoman Empire* (2 vols.; New York: Holmes & Meier, 1982).
7 E. Ashtor, "L'Apogée du commerce vénitien," in Hans-Georg Beck, Manoussos Manoussacas, and Agostino Pertusi, eds., *Venezia, Centro di Mediazone tra oriente e Occidente, Secoli XV–XVI* (Florence: L. S. Olshki, 1977).
8 Somewhat more seems to have been done by the Ottomans in the Balkans than in the Middle East; see Halil Inalcik, *The Ottoman Empire: The Classical Age, 1300–1460* (New York: Praeger, 1973), pp. 146–50.
9 For a partial list of plagues see Charles Issawi, *An Economic History of the Middle East and North Africa* (New York: Columbia University Press, 1982), pp. 97–9.
10 For examples of lack of interest see Charles Issawi, "Europe, the Middle East and the Shift in Power," reprinted in idem, *The Arab World's Legacy* (Princeton: Darwin Press, 1981), pp. 118–19; for an excellent general discussion, see Bernard Lewis, *The Muslim Discovery of Europe* (New York: W. W. Norton, 1982).
11 Lewis, pp. 50 and 306; Philip Hitti, *History of Syria, Including Lebanon and Palestine* (New York & London: Macmillan, 1951), pp. 676–7; Johannes Pedersen, *The Arabic Book* (Princeton: Princeton University Press, 1984), pp. 131–41.
12 Issawi, "Europe."
13 E. L. Jones, *The European Miracle* (Cambridge: Cambridge University press, 1981).
14 On this see Andrew Watson, *Agricultural Innovation in the Early Islamic World* (Cambridge and New York: Cambridge University Press, 1983). It may be noted that in England as early as the thirteenth century scientific treatises on agriculture and estate management began to be circulated; see George Trevelyan, *History of England* (London & New York: Longmans, Green, & Co., 1947), p. 153.
15 Carlo Cipolla, *Literacy and Development in the West* (Harmondsworth: Penguin, 1969), *passim*.
16 Carlo Cipolla, "The Italian and Iberian Peninsulas," *Cambridge Economic History of Europe*, Vol. III (1941), p. 413, and more generally pp. 408–19; see also Vol. IV (1967), chap. 8, and Vol. V (1977), chaps. 7 and 8.
17 Charles Issawi, "Why Japan?" in Ibrahim Ibrahim, ed., *Arab Resources* (Washington, D.C.: Center for Contemporary Arab Studies, 1983), pp. 283–300.
18 Edwin L. Harper, "Do We Need an Industrial Policy?" in Michael Wachter and Susan Wachter, eds., *Removing Obstacles to Economic Growth* (Philadelphia: University of Pennsylvania Press, 1984), p. 460.

19 C. E. Black *et al.*, *The Modernization of Japan and Russia* (New York: The Free Press, 1975), pp. 82–5, 106–9; Herbert Passin, *Society and Education in Japan* (New York: Teachers College, Columbia University, 1965), pp. 11–61; Nan [Ivan] Morris, *The Life of an Amorous Woman* (London, 1964), pp. 26–7.

20 Donald Keene, *the Japanese Discovery of Europe* (Stanford: Stanford University Press, 1969), *passim*.

21 For details see Issawi, "Why Japan," pp. 294–5.

22 See Jerome Blum, *The End of the Old Order in Europe* (Princeton: Princeton University Press, 1978), pp. 144–5; Issawi, *An Economic History*, p. 119.

23 Peter Lyashchenko, *History of the National Economy of Russia* (New York: Macmillan, 1949), pp. 269 and 833–55; Hermann Kellenbenz, "The Organization of Industrial Production," *Cambridge Economic History of Europe*, v, 529.

24 See Simone Blanc, "The Economic Policy of Peter the Great," in William Blackwell, ed., *Russian Economic Development from Peter the Great to Stalin* (New York: New Viewpoints, 1974), pp. 23–49.

25 See Arcadius Kahan, "Continuity in Economic Activity and Policy During the Post-Petrine Period," in Blackwell, *Russian Economic Development*, pp. 51–70.

26 For figures and details see Lyashchenko, pp. 292–304 and 329–39; Kahan, pp. 61–3.

27 See Lyashchenko, pp. 328–9 and 425–6; Roger Portal, "The Industrialization of Russia," *Cambridge Economic History of Europe*, Vol. vi (1965), pp. 801–63.

28 Joseph Roucek, ed., *Slavonic Encyclopaedia* (New York: Philosophical Library, 1949), p. 267; Richard Pipes, *Russia under the Old Regime* (New York: Weidenfeld & Nicolson, 1974), p. 123.

29 Lyashchenko, pp. 837–41; see also *Bol'shaia Sovetskaia Entsiklopedia* (2nd ed.; Moscow, 1949–57), s.v. "Lomonosov," "Ordin-Nashchokin," and "Pososhkov."

30 Joseph Schumpeter, *History of Economic Analysis* (New York: Oxford University Press, 1954), p. 193; Pipes, pp. 256–8.

31 Cipolla, *Literacy and Development*, p. 109.

32 V. K. Yatsumsky, "The Industrial Revolution in Russia," in Blackwell, *Russian Economic Development*, pp. 109–36; Lyashchenko, pp. 327–39.

33 Cipolla, *Literacy and Development*, p. 118.

34 See figures for 1862–1912 in John Lampe and Marvin Jackson, *Balkan Economic History, 1550–1950* (Bloomington: Indiana University Press, 1982), p. 188.

35 See Doreen Warriner, ed. *Contrasts in Emerging Societies* (Bloomington: Indiana University Press, 1965), p. 3 and *passim*; see also *La*

Révolution industrielle dans le Sud-Est européen (Sofia: Institut d'É-tudes Balkaniques, 1976), pp. 146–50 and *passim*.

36 Warriner, pp. 3–16 and *passim*; L. S. Stavrianos, *The Balkans since 1453* (New York: Dryden Press, 1958), pp. 296–7, 478–9; Lampe and Jackson, pp. 184–9.

37 For Serbia, see Warriner, pp. 302–8; for Bulgaria, ibid, pp. 255–6 and 273–5.

38 Bruce McGowan, *Economic Life in Ottoman Europe* (Cambridge and New York: Cambridge University Press, 1981); Lampe and Jackson, pp. 159–201.

39 Ibid., pp. 198–200, 305–6, and 369–75; and pp. 264–7 and 363.

40 Stavrianos, pp. 146–8.

41 See tables in Lampe and Jackson, pp. 502–4.

42 UNESCO, *Progress of Literacy in Various Countries* (Paris: UNESCO, 1953).

43 Marvin Jackson, "Comparing the Balkan Demographic Experience, 1860 to 1970," *Journal of European Economic History*, 14 (Fall 1985), 223–72.

44 See Jonathan Brown, *A Socioeconomic History of Argentina, 1776–1860* (Cambridge and New York: Cambridge University Press, 1979), pp. 225–34 and *passim*; also Laura Randall, *An Economic History of Argentina in the Twentieth Century* (New York: Columbia University Press, 1978).

45 D. A. Brading, *Miners and Merchants in Bourbon Mexico, 1763–1810* (Cambridge: Cambridge University Press, 1971), pp. 1–3; James Lockhart and Stuart Schwartz, *Early Latin America* (Cambridge and New York: Cambridge University Press, 1983), p. 36.

46 Brading, pp. 14–18; Lockhart and Schwartz, pp. 306–8.

47 Brading, pp. 18–19; Fernand Braudel, *The Perspective of the World* (New York: Harper & Row, 1984), p. 421.

48 Brading, pp. 94–100, 120–5, 131–9, 216; Lockhart and Schwartz, pp. 142–8.

49 Braudel, p. 421.

50 Lockhart and Schwartz, p. 342; John Chance, *Race and Class in Colonial Oaxaca* (Stanford: Stanford University Press, 1978), *passim*.

51 Brading, pp. 294–8.

52 John Lanning, *The University in the Kingdom of Guatemala* (Ithaca, N.Y.: Cornell University Press, 1955), p. 3; *Enciclopedia Universal Illustrada* (Barcelona & Madrid), s.v. "Mejico," "Peru."

53 John Elliott, *Imperial Spain, 1469–1716* (London: Edward Arnold, 1963), p. 118.

54 Lockhart and Schwartz, p. 411.

55 John Lanning, *The Eighteenth Century Enlightenment in the University*

of San Carlos de Guatemala (Ithaca, N.Y.: Cornell University Press, 1956).

56 Lockhart and Schwartz, pp. 344–6.

57 Evelyn Sakakida Rawski, *Education and Popular Literacy in Ching China* (Ann Arbor: University of Michigan Press, 1979), p. 23.

58 Issawi, *An Economic History, passim.*

59 On this subject, see Issawi, "Transformation of the Economic Position."

60 Richard Easterlin, "Why Isn't the Whole World Developed?," *Journal of Economic History*, 41 (March 1981), 1–17.

61 J. R. Hicks, *A Theory of Economic History* (Oxford: Clarendon Press, 1969), p. 39.

2 · The movement of labor in and out of the Middle East over the last two centuries: peasants, patterns, and policies*

ROGER OWEN
St. Antony's College, Oxford

Introduction

During the nineteenth century there were three great international movements which were central to the expansion of industrial Europe and the remaking of the non-European world: those of capital, of goods, and of people. Of these the first two have been endlessly studied and their role much theorized in order to explain (or sometimes to justify) the global process which different writers have characterized either as "development," "dependency," or the "development of underdevelopment," using such influential concepts as "imperialism," "unequal exchange," or trade as the "engine of growth."

Very much less care has been devoted to the third great movement: that of people. There is, it is true, a huge literature full of facts and figures, for example Thomas and Znaniecki's monumental *The Polish Peasant in Europe and America*, or Ferenczi and Willcox's two-volume study, *International Migration*, for the International Labor Office in Geneva.[1] It is also true, however, that such studies have produced very little in the way of general theory. This has probably something to do with the many difficulties inherent in finding all the necessary information about the migrants themselves and, in particular, what jobs they took and whether or not they stayed in their new place of work or eventually returned home. But it is also the result of approaches which have tended to see the phenomenon within too narrow a frame of reference, as can be seen by a brief examination of the literature generated by the two great waves of migration in the late nineteenth and mid-twentieth centuries. In the first case, analysis of the movement which took over 32 million people from Europe to North America and the white British colonies between 1881 and 1915, tended to treat the phenomenon as one involving persons in search of a new life rather than a new job.[2] And this led, naturally, to a situation in which the study of migration became largely a branch of demography, and then of sociology, in which there was a major focus on such notions as the "melting pot," ethnicity and racialism, and intercommunal relations.

In contrast to this, writers on the second great wave of the 1950s and 1960s, which brought 15 million or so people to Western Europe from the Mediterranean region and from countries that were once part of Western empires, have generally concentrated their attention on the migrants as a form of mobile labor, or simply as a factor of production, with a consequent employment of such notions as "reserve army" or the creation of a new "proletariat."[3] And, again to speak very generally, these writers appear to have been remarkably unconcerned about who the migrants were, where they came from, or the mechanisms by which they were forced to abandon their previous existence. In this they share some of the negative features of the writers on the first wave: an unwillingness to distinguish between the migrants as workers or as people, and an overwhelming interest in what happens to them in their new life to the exclusion of what types of persons they were to begin with. Perhaps for this same reason they fail to raise many of the most important questions and seem to ignore one of the major lessons from history, which is that most waves of migration have their own special character and their own particular dynamic.

There is one recent trend, however, which, so it seems to me, has started to become much more fruitful, and that is the focus on the migrants as mainly rural people – and often peasants.[4] This is part of the more general interest in the global impact of economic change on the peasant way of life and in the mechanisms by which the peasantry is squeezed out of its agrarian heartland and recruited for (largely urban) employment. In the particular context of the study of migration this had led to the very important discovery that when looked at from the point of view of their rural origins, many migrant workers do not look quite so much like emerging proletarians (even when they stay in Western Europe for long periods) as what Shanin has termed "peasant workers," whose situation is very much conditioned by the fact that they retain certain significant social, cultural, and often economic ties with their home village.[5]

The centrality of this phenomenon can certainly be deduced from many of the statistics for both the nineteenth and the twentieth century: for example, according to Thomas and Znaniecki, at least half the Polish peasants who went off to find work in the United

States between 1897 and 1915 returned home in spite of the increasingly harsh conditions in Poland, while a similar story seems to have been true for migrants from the Indian subcontinent at about the same period.[6] It can also be observed in some of the more autobiographical or impressionistic literature, for example in Carlo Levi's *Christ Stopped at Eboli*, where he notes that in the 1930s it was New York, not Rome, which was the capital city for poor migrants from the little town of Gagliano in the Italian south – but in a special kind of way.

As a place to work, it [New York] is indifferent to them; they live there as they would live anywhere else, like animals harnessed to a wagon, heedless of the street where they must pull it. But as an earthly paradise, Jerusalem the Golden, it is so sacred as to be untouchable; a man can only gaze at it, even when he is there on the spot with no hope of attainment. The peasants who emigrate to America remain just what they always were, many stay there and their children become Americans, but the rest who come back twenty years later are just the same as when they went away. In three months they forget the few words of English they ever learned, they slough off the few superficial habits and are the same peasants they were before, like stones which a rushing stream has long coursed over but which dry out under the first warm rays of the sun. In America they live apart, among themselves; for years they eat nothing but bread, just as they did in Gagliano, saving all their meagre earnings. They live next to the earthly paradise, but they dare not enter.[7]

Levi's description may well be truer of Europeans than of some non-Europeans, and it may also be truer of the past than the present. Nevertheless, it does help to focus on certain very important questions which are also implicit in much of the other literature on the rural origins of today's migrants. For example: why do some stay in Europe or America, in spite of their lack of integration into the social and cultural life of the metropolis, and others not? And why do some of those who return go to their original villages while others prefer to move to the nearest large town? Clearly, the answers lie just as much in the study of the process of economic transformation in the Third World as in that in the advanced industrial countries.

In what follows I want to use some of these notions to structure an examination of some of the most significant migrations in and out of the Middle East during the nineteenth and twentieth centuries, paying special attention to the following hypotheses: (1) Most migrants have been rural in origin. (2) Most individual migrations consist of an implicit cycle of movement away from the village and then return, even if this cycle is broken at some stage (for example, when a migrant decides to stay permanently abroad) or is extended over a very long period of time. (3) Each wave of migration has its own history.

I should add that I will concentrate only on those movements which involved migration for employment and so exclude other large movements of population where the motive was largely political, for example, the arrival in the Ottoman Empire of some 2.5 million Muslim refugees from southern Russia between 1854 and 1895, or the vast exchange of peoples between Greece and Turkey at the end of World War I.[8] I will also exclude reference to the important build-up of European populations in the countries of the Middle East and North Africa during the colonial period.

The Middle East in the nineteenth and early twentieth centuries

It goes without saying that, for most of the Middle East in the nineteenth century, the vast bulk of the population lived in the rural areas and earned its living from some type of pastoralism or settled agriculture. In these circumstances the main opportunity for migration for employment within the region itself was provided not by the very few large urban centers but by differences in local patterns of crop rotations, which provided jobs for certain peasant cultivators during their own off season. A good example of this is the seasonal movement of many hundreds of thousands of men from Upper Egypt every summer in the late nineteenth century to work at picking or transporting cotton, or canal-cleaning in the Delta at the time of year when there was no possibility for activity in their own fields.[9] Other movements involved men from the hilly areas of Syria/Lebanon/Palestine or of northeast Morocco down on to the surrounding plains for the harvest.[10]

There were, however, at least three significant migrations of Middle Eastern peasants outside the region and I will mention these briefly in turn. Far and away the most important in terms of size was that which took peasants from the north Persian provinces across the border to find work in the growth areas of the rapidly developing Russian economy, for example, the oil industry at Baku, the fishing industry on the Caspian Sea, or the large number of roads, railways, and other public works projects. According to Abdulaev, quoted in Issawi's *The Economic History of Iran*, there were very few north Persian workers at the end of the nineteenth century who had not spent some time in Russia.[11] Abdulaev also posits that the reason for this was the lack of alternative employment prospects in the area, either inside or outside agriculture. Meanwhile, the official Russian statistics for legal movement across Russia's southern borders show that the number of migrants entering the country increased from 67,000 in 1900 to 275,000 in 1913.[12] The fact that roughly similar numbers also left Russia each year testifies to the seasonal or short-term nature of this phenomenon. It is also said that some 200,000 Persians entered Russia without permits in 1911.[13] Estimates of the remittances sent back to Persia by these workers run up to something like 14 million rubles just before World War I, the equivalent of $7 million.[14]

In terms of numbers the second largest migration was that of Syrians, Palestinians, and Lebanese, most of them to North or South America. As the majority were Christians, it is likely that some of them were driven by fears of religious persecution – particularly after the Lebanese massacres of 1860 – or by a desire to escape more troubles and perhaps conscription into the Ottoman army after 1908. But there is also considerable testimony as to the role of rural poverty and of population pressure up in the hills, where agriculture was generally confined to the crops that could be grown on narrow mountainside terraces.[15] Figures to illustrate the size of this movement are subject to a wide margin of error, the more so as Syrians arriving in the United States were all classified as Ottomans before 1914 on the basis of their passports.[16] Arthur Ruppin, writing in 1916, reported that the local authorities informed him that some 100,000 persons had left the mutasarraflik of Mount Lebanon before 1915, while nearly as many again may have migrated from other parts of Syria and Palestine.[17] Ruppin also provides testimony that a large part of this migration was for temporary employment, and he estimates that something like a third to a half of the migrants returned to the Middle East after they had earned "enough money."[18] Finally, Ruppin's inquiries at local banks revealed that just before World War I, remittances sent back to Syria and Lebanon were running at some 30 million francs ($6 million) a year.[19]

The third migratory process was very much smaller and involved some 10,000 Algerians (almost all Berbers from Kabyle) who went to France between 1906/7 and 1914. Unlike the other two migrations, this was very much a "colonial" type of movement, with the initial impetus for recruitment coming from French employers in the metropolis and the whole process monitored by the Algerian and French governments.[20] But there was certainly a "push" factor in terms of the well-documented poverty and land shortage in the Algerian rural areas and the difficulty of obtaining satisfactory work in the European-dominated towns.[21] Demand for Algerian labor increased further during World War I, and by 1918 there were an estimated 30,000 workers in France remitting something like 38 million francs ($7.6 million) a year.[22]

Migration continued from the Middle East after World War I but at a somewhat reduced rate. To begin with, many of the former labor-importing countries began to introduce restrictions on entry, particularly Russia after the revolution and the United States with the Immigration Act of 1921. Later on, the deteriorating economic conditions during the early years of the World Depression of the 1930s made migration a much less attractive option, and in several Middle Eastern countries there was probably a net inward migration as the number of those returning began to exceed the number of those who wanted to leave. According to figures collected by the French Mandatory authorities the numbers of migrants leaving Syria and Lebanon varied between 11,000 and 16,000 in the mid-1920s.[23] Given the increasing difficulty of gaining admission to the United States, the majority now went to South America or to West Africa.[24] With the onset of the World Depression the numbers fell away to some 2,000 to 4,000 in the mid-1930s, probably somewhat less than those whom economic hardship forced to return.[25]

As for Algeria, while most of the wartime migrants went back home after 1918, leaving perhaps only 12,000 by 1920, another large surge took place which took the numbers up to 100,000 by 1924.[26] After that, however, any further movement was curtailed, first by government regulation and after that by the French economic crisis, so that by 1936 there were only 36,000 North Africans in France (the majority Algerians), while their number shrank still further during World War II.[27] So ended the first period of migration from the Middle East, a process that has been well characterized by Abdelmalek Sayed as one in which the primary motive force was the struggle of a poor peasantry to survive and find a means of keeping itself going in its rural environment.[28] I will now attempt to examine some of the principal features of the second, larger wave of peasant migration, which began with the West European economic recovery of the 1950s.

**Middle Eastern migration to Europe during the economic boom of
the 1950s and 1960s**

Once its postwar economic recovery began to gather momentum in
the 1950s Western Europe soon began to experience significant
shortages of labor which were met, first, from adjacent countries
like East Germany, Italy, and Spain, and then increasingly from
Turkey and North Africa. As a result, by 1973, there were some
675,000 Turks working in the European Economic Community
countries, mostly in West Germany, and an almost equal number of
North Africans, most of them Algerians, at work in France.[29] The
value of remittances was also very large, amounting to some $300
million a year for the Algerians in 1973, according to a report by the
Organization for Economic Cooperation and Development, and
nearly $1,500 million for the Turks in 1974 – or almost the same as
the country's entire merchandise exports.[30]

The migrations from Europe and from the Middle East had much
in common. They consisted largely of rural people, but in such
numbers that the impact on peasant society was very much greater
than before World War II. No longer was it a question of simple
survival but one in which movement to Western Europe was seen as
the major avenue towards realizing a general aspiration towards a
higher standard of living, which the new economic conditions in
their own home country both "authorized and prevented."[31] An
increasing number of workers began to send for their families to
come live with them. And while ties with their own home villages
generally remained close, the majority of migrants either chose to
stay for longer and longer periods in Europe, perhaps waiting until
some specific aspiration, like their children's education, had been
achieved or, if they did return, moving at once to a large town where
employment prospects were better and the standard of welfare
service much higher than in the rural areas. The result was that the
new pattern of migration became part of a specific process of a
de-peasantization in which the migrant himself was no longer a
peasant but not quite yet a worker.[32]

A second characteristic which both the Algerian and the Turkish
migration shared was their trajectories, beginning with a period of
explosive growth in numbers, then experiencing a few years of
ever-tightening control, before coming to an almost complete halt
in the early 1970s as a result of a ban on further recruitment. In the
case of the Turks, a ban was imposed by the German government in
1973; in the case of the Algerians, by their own government in the

same year. There was, however, one significant difference: while the Algerian migration began by being largely uncontrolled, according to the general pattern of movement from former colonies to the metropolis, that of the Turks was subject to minute agreement by the governments concerned from the very start. This was the result of the Turko-German bilateral agreement of 1961, which standardized recruitment practices and provided for the establishment of new institutions to look after the welfare of the migrant workers.[33]

Just as important for the purposes of the present argument, the Turko-German agreement was based on an implicit model of the process of labor migration between rich and poor countries, which was soon proved to be incorrect. Initially it was assumed that both sides could maximize their benefits quite easily, the Germans by providing themselves with a cheap source of temporary labor without incurring any major social cost, the Turks by obtaining a regular flow of returning workers with skills and capital to invest in industrial or agricultural enterprise.[34] But the majority of Turks preferred to continue to reside in Germany even when unemployed, and the German government was soon forced to change its policies to cope with the increasing Turkish population, first by banning further recruitment, then by trying to devise measures to provide for those Turks and their families who showed little willingness to return home. The latter proved extremely difficult, however. First, there were deep divisions within German society about whether the government should aim at integrating the Turks into the local population or at treating them as, in some ways, an alien community with its own economic and cultural norms. Second, the problem was made more complicated by the fact that the Turks showed all the ambiguity of a group that thought itself as part worker/part peasant, being anxious to stay on in Germany in the medium term for certain specific reasons (such as the receipt of a pension), but still planning to return to Turkey at some unspecified time in the future and thus anxious to maintain close links with the mother country. In more recent years the French government has had to grapple with almost the same problem with respect to the Algerians.

The Middle East in the oil boom of the 1970s: new patterns of labor migration

The third and last major movement of Middle Eastern migration is that associated with the oil boom that began in the Gulf states, Iraq,

Libya, and Saudi Arabia in the early 1970s. There are no proper figures for this, given the general reluctance of Middle Eastern governments to collect them, but it would seem that the numbers of Arab migrant workers involved may be somewhere in the region of 6 million, half of them in Saudi Arabia and the Gulf, the other half in Libya and Iraq. As far as the origin of immigrants is concerned, Egypt was far and away the largest labor exporter, with some 3 million workers abroad in the early 1980s, followed by the two Yemens and then Jordan and West Bank Palestinians.[35] Figures for remittances are also difficult to establish because so many of them are transmitted via unofficial channels. But as far as those sent through the banking systems are concerned, the World Bank gives $2 billion for Egypt in 1982, and $1 billion each for Jordan and North Yemen.[36]

The reasons for this vast movement of labor were twofold. On the one hand, the major oil exporters (with the exception of Iraq) were countries with small populations, a very low labor participation ratio, and few of the skills needed to develop their economies to provide themselves with advanced social welfare services on the Kuwait model. On the other hand, profits from oil were so large and the need to spend them quickly so great that Gulf wages soon exceeded those of their poorer neighbors by anything up to a ratio of 20:1.[37] Meanwhile, countries like Egypt during the rule of President Sadat came to see remittances as a major source of foreign currency and removed most of the barriers and controls to the free movement of workers or their accumulated funds. Within a few years the migration of labor had become a flood which affected almost every corner of every Middle Eastern economy, profoundly changing employment practices, wage rates, and consumption patterns in a way that governments were both unwilling and unable to control.

Apart from its vast size, the new movement of labor within the Middle East had a number of important features. First, it was largely unplanned and unorganized. For the most part Arab workers found jobs by means of personal or local connections; for the most part they were employed by private individuals or companies to whom the local states delegated a major responsibility for ensuring that regulations governing their residence and their work were respected. This latter system, known informally as the "kafeel" or patronage system, made it very difficult for states either to control the flow of labor or to devise proper methods for planning its future growth. By the same token, Arab workers received very little protection either from the labor laws of the host state or from their own government. Second, because of the local lack of labor of all types, the flow of migrants involved men with every kind of skill from the highest professional qualifications to nothing more than their own brute strength. Given the fact that the largest demand was for construction workers, it would seem reasonable to suppose that the majority of Arab migrants were unskilled or semiskilled persons of rural origin. But in this case, at least, the peasant component was heavily admixed with men from the towns and cities.

Some of the same characteristics are also apparent in the case of the other great flow of migrant labor to the oil-rich states, that of men and women from almost every country in Asia. Once again, there are no adequate statistics, while the few figures given by the donor governments almost always tend to be larger than those provided by the receiving states. One good guess might be that there were some 4 million Asian workers employed in the Gulf, Saudi Arabia, and Iraq in the early 1980s, perhaps half of them from Pakistan.[38] As in the case of the Arabs, a significant proportion, possibly as much as a third, were employed in some aspect of the construction industry, many of them as unskilled laborers.[39] Given the continued importance of the agricultural sector as a source of employment in most Asian economies, it may also be supposed that a majority of these workers were of rural origin.

There are, however, some significant differences between the Arab and the Asian migration.[40] One is that, for the most part, Asian workers were recruited by contractors or employment agencies to whom they had usually to pay a fee. The second is that the Asian states were much more directly involved in trying to safeguard the welfare of their migrant workers even if, as often happened, they were much more successful in looking after their rights before they left their home country than while they were at work in the Middle East itself. Most Asian states have established a system for licensing recruitment agencies and for regulating the commissions they charge. They have also tried to ensure that departing workers have proper contracts and some knowledge of the conditions they must expect to face. Finally, most of them have appointed labor attachés at their Gulf embassies and consulates, even though there are enormous obstacles in the way of their making contact with their own nationals and in investigating complaints.

Given the enormous variety of foreign labor employed in the oil-exporting states and the problems in obtaining adequate information, further generalization is difficult. There are two areas, however, about which it might be useful to say more. The first concerns the future of foreign labor migrants in the oil-exporting states now that oil revenues have shrunk to something like a third of their 1981 levels. In spite of repeated newspaper stories of the wholescale lay-off of foreign labor, there is good reason to believe that the situation is not as desperate as it is often painted. For one thing, most of the oil exporters have large reserves, both public and private, accumulated during the boom years of the late 1970s and early 1980s, and these have allowed investment and employment to continue at rates not much less than their previous peak, particularly in Saudi Arabia.[41] For another, Gulf governments have been unwilling to run what they see as dangerous political risks in getting rid of Arab labor. They are anxious both to maintain a high level of services for their own citizens and to prevent the growth of dissatisfaction among communities like those of the Palestinians who might bitterly resist anything that looks like a policy of mass deportation. Some proof of this comes from the fact that, at the time of writing (January 1986) there is still a net outward migration of Palestinians and Jordanians from Jordan in spite of the cutbacks in Saudi Arabia and the Gulf. What seems to have happened is that many Arab workers have been forced to accept quite a severe cut in salary whenever their contracts have come up for renewal. The same thing is likely to be happening to the Asians, particularly in view of the enormous competition between exporting countries to continue to send workers. As Gulf wages and salaries started off at such a high level compared with other Arab and Asian ones, there is obviously a lot of room for reduction before the cuts become unacceptable.

The second area concerns the conditions under which foreign labor is employed in the Gulf, as well as, to some extent, in Libya and Iraq. This is of importance for general humanitarian reasons and also because it raises important questions about the policies of the labor-importing countries towards what may be a large permanent resident foreign community that will simply not go away. At the moment the situation of foreigners, whether Arabs or Asians, leaves a great deal to be desired. They are largely unprotected in their workplace, without the right to organize unions and subject to local labor laws which leave many important categories uncovered (for example, domestic servants) and which are administered by local labor courts and ministries of labor that have not shown themselves active in looking after the interests of their own nationals, let alone foreigners. Foreign workers are also discrimi-

nated against in various ways in that they cannot own property, set
up their own business, or enjoy most of the other rights taken for
granted by local citizens. Perhaps worst of all, they have no surety as
to their residence, can be deported if the work permit runs out, and
must always be uncertain about getting back into the country once
they have left it for a temporary visit back home. Such a situation
might have had some justification while the governments and
peoples of the oil-exporting states believed, wrongly, that their
need for foreign labor was only a short-lived, temporary phenomenon. But now that they have recognized that they will not be able
to do without such assistance for a long time to come there is every
reason for them to try to place their foreign residents under some
less precarious regime. The problem here is that their own people
have become so used to the exercise of financial and other privileges
based on their own monopoly of certain basic rights (for example,
ownership of houses and other property), that they are most unwilling to extend them to a wider circle than at present.

Conclusion

In so brief a space it is only possible to touch upon a few of the larger
themes connected with the history of labor migration in and out of
the Middle East and its proper analysis. At root what I have suggested is twofold. First, that the process of this migration has proceeded in terms of short bursts of activity, each with its own
dynamic and each being brought to an end by some combination of
economic and political cut-off. I have also argued that the history of
Middle Eastern migration has shown an extension of the degree of
involvement of the peasant sector, from one in which the search for
overseas employment was part of a simple strategy for survival, to
one in which whole sections of a rural population came to see
employment abroad as providing access to a standard of living and
of welfare which they perceived as modern. In the latter case,
however, they still give themselves the option of choosing either to
become modern or to return to the village from which the whole
process started.

My second suggestion is that the ambiguous nature of the rural
migrations I have described, based at least initially on peasant
resistance to full proletarianization, has constantly defeated those
in government who hoped to use it as a short-term expedient which
could then be easily dispensed with, leaving them with the extremely difficult problem of dealing with a semipermanent resident

community which neither wants to be fully assimilated nor to go home. Perhaps only in countries like the United States, with its huge population, its toleration of cultural pluralism, and last but not least, its invention of the concept of the "green card," have the explosive tensions inherent in this situation been largely defused.

NOTES

* I intend this short essay to be a complement to Charles Issawi's treatment of the same subject in his *An Economic History of the Middle East and North Africa* (New York: Columbia University Press, 1982), ch. 5.

1 William Isaac Thomas and F. Znaniecki, *The Polish Peasant in Europe and America* (5 vols.; Boston: Graham Press, 1918–20). Imre Ferenczi, ed., *International Migrations*, Vol. I, with introduction and notes by W. F. Willcox (New York: National Bureau of Economic Research, 1929), and W. F. Willcox, ed., *International Migrations*, Vol. II (New York: National Bureau of Economic Research, 1931).

2 Figures from A. G. Kenwood and A. L. Lougheed, *The Growth of the International Economy 1820–1960* (London: George Allen and Unwin; Sydney: Australasian Publishing Co., 1971), p. 60.

3 Figures from Jonathan Power (in collaboration with Anna Hardman), *Western Europe's Migrant Workers* (London: Minority Rights Group, n.d.), pp. 7, 9.

4 This idea is forcefully presented by Teodor Shanin in "The Peasants are Coming: Migrants Who Labour, Peasants Who Travel and Marxists Who Write," *Race and Class*, 19 (Winter 1978), 281–6.

5 Ibid., pp. 284–6.

6 Thomas and Znaniecki, *The Polish Peasant*, Vol. v, 29. Imre Ferenczi and W. R. Willcox, eds., *International Migrations*, Vol. I (2nd ed.; New York, London, and Paris: Gordon, 1969), p. 143.

7 Carlo Levi, *Christ Stopped at Eboli* (Harmondsworth etc: Penguin, 1982), pp. 121–2.

8 The figures for Muslim refugees came from Stanford J. Shaw and Ezel Kural Shaw, *History of the Ottoman Empire and Modern Turkey*, Vol. II, *Reform Revolution and the Republic: The Rise of Modern Turkey 1808–1975* (Cambridge: Cambridge University Press, 1977), p. 116.

9 Y. Artin, "Essai sur les causes du renchérissement de la vie matérielle au Caire dans le courant du XIXe siècle (1800–1917)," *Mémoires présentés à l'Institut égyptien*, Vol. v (Cairo: Institut Egyptien, 1907), p. 87.

10 Roger Owen, *The Middle East in the World Economy 1800–1914* (London etc: Methuen, 1981), p. 245; David Seddon, "Labour Migration and Agricultural Development in Northeast Morocco: 1870–1970, pt. 1," *The Maghreb Review*, 4 (May–June 1979), 69.

11 Z. Z. Abdulaev, translated in Charles Issawi, *The Economic History of Iran 1800–1914* (Chicago: University of Chicago Press, 1971), pp. 50–2.

12 Marvin L. Entner, *Russo-Persian Commercial Relations, 1828–1914*, University of Florida Monographs, Social Sciences No. 28 (Gainesville: University of Florida Pres, 1965), p. 60.

13 Ibid.

14 Ibid., pp. 60–1.

15 For example, "La question syrienne," *Revue du Monde Musulman*, 2 (June–July 1907), 520, or Père J. A. Jaussen, *Coutumes palestiniennes*, Vol. I, *Naplouse et son district* (Paris: P. Geuthner, 1927), p. 20.

16 Philip M. Kayal and Joseph M. Kayal, *The Syrian-Lebanese in America* ([New York]: Twayne Publ., 1975), p. 67.

17 A. Ruppin, translated in Charles Issawi, ed. *The Economic History of the Middle East 1800–1914* (Chicago: University of Chicago Press, 1966), pp. 271–2.

18 Ibid., p. 271.

19 Ibid., p. 272. See also Arthur Ruppin, *Syria: An Economic Survey* (New York: Provisional Zionist Committee, 1918), p. 12.

20 Charles-Robert Ageron, *Les Algériens musulmans et la France (1871–1919)*, Vol. II (Paris: Presses Universitaires de France, 1968), pp. 854–5.

21 Ibid., pp. 846–7, 852–4.

22 Ibid., pp. 857–8.

23 *La Syrie et le Liban sous l'occupation et le Mandat français 1919–1927* (Paris, Nancy, Strasbourg: Berger-Levrault, n.d.), p. 312.

24 Ibid., p. 313.

25 United Kingdom, Naval Intelligence Division, *Syria* (April 1943), pp. 206–7.

26 Mohamed Mehani, "North African Migration to Europe," in United Nations Economic Commission for West Asia, *International Migration in the Arab World*, Vol. I (Beirut: UNECWA, 1982), p. 148.

27 Ibid., pp. 148–9.

28 Abdelmalek Sayed, "Les trois âges de l'émigration algérienne," *Actes de la Recherche en Sciences Sociales*, 15 (June 1977), 61–4.

29 Power, *Western Europe's Migrant Workers*, Table 1.

30 Issawi, *An Economic History of the Middle East and North Africa*, pp. 87–8.

31 The phrase comes from Sayed, "Les trois âges," pp. 61–4.

32 Ibid., p. 67.

33 Nermin Abadan-Unat, "Turkish Migration to Europe, 1960–1975," in N. Abadan-Unat, *Turkish Workers in Europe* (Leiden: Brill, 1976).

34 Nermin Abadan-Unat, "Turkish Migration to Europe and the Middle East: Its Impact on Social Legislation and Social Structure," unpublished paper presented to the Conference of Social Legislation and Social Structure in the Contemporary Near and Middle East, Rabat, Morocco, 25–9 September 1981, p. 2 (mimeographed).

35 Given the absence of official statistics these figures can only be based on informed guesses. For the sources of guesses for the Gulf, see Roger

Owen, *Migrant Workers in the Gulf* (London: Minority Rights Group. n.d.), Appendix Table 1. The estimates for Iraq and Libya are based on the assumption that there might well have been between 2 and 2.5 million Egyptian workers in these two countries, plus smaller numbers of other Arabs. For support for the latter guesses see statement by Egyptian prime minister reported in *Egyptian Gazette*, 17 February 1983, when he speaks of "three million Egyptians working abroad."

36 The World Bank, *World Development Report 1984* (New York: Oxford University Press, 1984), Table 14.

37 This is a very rough calculation based on the figures for the wages of Egyptian teachers and unskilled laborers to be found in the sources cited in Owen, *Migrant Workers*, p. 4.

38 Ibid., Appendix Table 2.

39 Based on Antoine B. Zahlan's figures for employment in the Arab construction industry, "Migratory Labour in the Arab World," *Third World Quarterly*, 6 (October 1984), p. 985.

40 See Owen, *Migrant Workers*, pp. 5–6 and 8–11, for a further discussion of this subject.

41 Support for this argument comes from Naiem A. Sherbiny, *Labour and Capital Flows in the Arab World: A Critical View*, IBK Papers no. 16 (Kuwait: The Industrial Bank of Kuwait, February 1985), pp. 66–9.

3 · Oil and economic development in the Middle East

HOMA KATOUZIAN

University of Kent at Canterbury

This paper is in three parts. Section 1 briefly presents the historical background to recent developments in the Middle East. Section 2 concentrates on some key issues in the theory and practice of economic development in the oil-exporting countries of the Middle East. Section 3 consists of an appraisal of the interdependencies of the Middle Eastern oil economies with the rest of the world.

1. Some perspectives on earlier developments

Oil was discovered in the Middle East at the beginning of the twentieth century. The first major oil discovery was in Iran, and the D'Arcy concession provided the basis for the concessionary system elsewhere in the Middle East, which survived until the 1950s. In the later period, and as a consequence of the Anglo-Iranian oil dispute, the concessionary system was replaced by the system of consortia, although all the main upstream and downstream operations remained in the hands of the major international oil companies. Finally, the developments of the late 1960s and the 1970s resulted in the full control of the producing countries themselves.[1]

In the 1900s the price of a barrel of oil was $1.20; in 1958, it was $2.08. This was reduced to $1.92 in the following year, bringing the price slightly below its 1953 level (see Table 1). A further price reduction in 1960 was the immediate reason behind the formation of the Organization of Petroleum Exporting Countries. OPEC's original aim was the modest one of stabilizing the nominal price of oil. In fact, the nominal price fell further in the following year, but remained stable for the rest of the 1960s (see Table 1).

In the first decade of its existence, OPEC did not have much influence in the major oil operations. Member countries still negotiated directly with the operating countries. Although the real price

44

Table 1 · Crude oil prices Saudi Arabia, 1953–1977 and nominal
and real oil prices, 1974–1980 (dollars per barrel)

Year	Crude Oil Prices (Ras Tanura) (1)	Nominal Oil Prices (2)	Real Oil Prices[a] (3)	Real Oil Prices[b] (4)	Real Oil Prices[c] (5)
1953	1.93	–	–	–	–
1954	1.93	–	–	–	–
1955	1.93	–	–	–	–
1956	1.93	–	–	–	–
1957	2.02	–	–	–	–
1958	2.08	–	–	–	–
1959	1.92	–	–	–	–
1960	1.86	–	–	–	–
1961	1.80	–	–	–	–
1962	1.80	–	–	–	–
1963	1.80	–	–	–	–
1964	1.80	–	–	–	–
1965	1.80	–	–	–	–
1966	1.80	–	–	–	–
1967	1.80	–	–	–	–
1968	1.80	–	–	–	–
1969	1.80	–	–	–	–
1970	1.80	–	–	–	–
1971	2.19	–	–	–	–
1972	2.46	–	–	–	–
1973	3.29	–	–	–	–
1974	11.58	9.56	9.56	9.56	10.45
1975	11.53	10.46	9.39	8.99	10.72
1976	12.38	11.51	9.51	7.66	11.51
1977	13.00	12.40	9.43	9.03	11.48
1978	–	12.70	8.95	8.12	10.24
1979	–	17.84	11.37	10.11	11.54
1980	–	28.67	16.24	14.35	17.27

[a] Deflated for inflation in OECD countries.
[b] Deflated for inflation rates in OECD countries plus dollar fluctuations *vis-à-vis* major currencies.
[c] Deflated for the inflation rate of OPEC import prices.

Sources, col. (1): M. W. Khouja and P. G. Saddler, *The Economy of Kuwait* (London: Macmillan, 1979) (original source: IMF, *International Financial Statistics*, 1977).
cols. (2)–(4): Yusuf Sayigh, Arab Oil Policies in the 1970s (London: Croom Helm, 1983), Table 4.1 (original source: OAPEC, *Secretary General's Seventh Annual Report*, 1977).
col. (5): UNCTAD, *Trade and Development Report*, 1982.

of oil was declining, the continuing increase in the world demand for crude made it possible for the oil countries of the Middle East and elsewhere to benefit from steadily increasing revenues in consequence of rising export quantities. Between 1961 and 1969 there was almost a threefold increase in the oil exports of seven Arab countries – Algeria, Iraq, Kuwait, Libya, Qatar, Saudi Arabia, and the United Arab Emirates – while their revenues increased at a slightly faster rate (see Table 2).

The Libyan price increase in 1970 led to the Tehran–Tripoli

Table 2 · Oil production and revenues of seven Arab oil-exporting countries[a]: selected years

Year	Production (1000 b/d)	Total Revenue ($ million)	Revenue per barrel
1961	4,748.5	1,190.2	0.69
1965	8,170.5	2,159.8	0.72
1969	12,549.6	3,937.6	0.86
1973	18,009.8	12,491.4	1.90
1974	17,723.3	51,499.3	2.96
1977	19,176.1	77,812.8	11.12
1980	19,233.8	204,244.0	29.01

[a] Algeria, Iraq, Kuwait, Libya, Qatar, Saudi Arabia, UAE
Source: Yusif Sayigh, *Arab Oil Policies in the 1970s* (London: Croom Helm, 1983), Table 4.2.

agreement between the companies and the producing countries, and this indicated the way to a substantial price increase. The fourfold price rise of 1973–4 was, however, as dramatic as it was unexpected. The long-term shift in the balance of power between the major producing and consuming countries, the dollar devaluations of 1971 and 1973, the Arab–Israeli war of October 1973 – and the subsequent Arab oil boycott – provided the background, pretext, and atmosphere for a dramatic price increase. This is known as the first "oil shock."[2]

In 1974 it looked as if oil prices were set for a continuous increase, so that at least the real price of oil would be maintained. There were a number of arguments in favor of OPEC limitations of production. First, given the low estimates of price elasticity of demand for crude at the time, price increases would raise nominal revenues. Second, production limitations would reduce the rate of resource depletion. Third, and by reducing crude exports, production limitations would also diminish the balance of payments surpluses and the problems associated with their deployment in foreign aid and investment.

In practice, OPEC's pricing policy since 1974 has been unanimous: when the nominal prices were rising, "the moderates," especially Saudi Arabia and Kuwait, frequently disagreed with "the radicals" – mainly Libya and Iraq, but occasionally Iran as well – over the rate of price increases.

Politics apart, price moderation for countries like Saudi Arabia, which have large proven reserves and relatively limited absorptive capacity, made economic and business sense. On the whole, "the moderates" managed to prevail until 1979, when in consequence of the Iranian revolution (leading to a substantial decline in Iranian exports, as well as panic buying), OPEC's reference price was revised to $34. This is known as the second oil shock. The result was a significant increase in the real price of oil, after a few years of steady decline (see Table 1).

In the early 1980s, a number of short- and long-term factors reversed the price trend: the world economic recession, energy conservation in consuming countries, and the substitution of other feedstocks (notably natural gas) for oil. In 1979, the OPEC volume of exports was 31 million barrels per day; in 1983, it had fallen to 17 million. The third oil shock followed in January 1983, when OPEC reduced its reference price to $29 per barrel.[3]

The years 1984 and 1985 (up to the time of writing the present paper) saw competition among OPEC members for increasing these sales, sometimes beyond the agreed OPEC quotas. Sales of crude at a discount, barter agreements, and other forms of non-price competition became regular features of international oil deals. But OPEC's reference price was maintained at $29 per barrel at its January 1984 conference. The latest price decrease (January 1985) was precipitated by a price reduction, in October 1984, by two non-OPEC members (Norway and Britain), and was followed by a bigger price cut by Nigeria which is a member of OPEC. The crisis led to the OPEC emergency meetings of October and December 1984, followed by the annual meeting in January 1985, at which, finally, OPEC resolved to reduce the reference price of Arabian light crude from $29 to $28 by a majority decision.

2. Oil revenues and development policy: problems of theory and practice

Capital has two faces: finance and machinery; the accumulation of capital for economic development has two aspects: domestic and foreign. The oil revenues combine these various characteristics of capital and its accumulation: they increase the country's financial resources in terms of both domestic and foreign currency, and they present the country with the problem of choice between present and future consumption, and domestic and foreign investment. The extent and significance of the problem, however, vary from one oil country to another.

In general, two types of oil economies may be distinguished: the relatively large and agricultural type, and the relatively small and non-agricultural category. The first group consists of countries which have an extensive traditional agricultural sector, and hence a relatively large population. By contrast, the second group of oil countries has a small or negligible agricultural sector and a relatively small population base. In the Middle East, Iran and Iraq are examples of the agricultural type, and Kuwait and UAE of the non-agricultural group of countries. Libya and Saudi Arabia do not exactly fit either of these two groups, but are closer to the non-agricultural countries in their non-oil resource endowments.

This simple classification has certain implications for the domestic economic development and external relations of the oil-exporting countries. First, per-capita incomes in the non-agricultural countries tend to be larger, sometimes considerably, than in the agricultural economies. This may make the problem of income redistribution somewhat less urgent, but it implies a lower absorptive capacity, and a larger balance-of-payments surplus. The accumulation of larger surpluses, in turn, poses questions about their deployment in other countries, the levels of production of crude, and the country's attitude to price change. Secondly, the non-agricultural oil economy would be relatively more dependent on migrant workers, both skilled and unskilled, because of its smaller population base and its lower rate of accumulation of physical and human capital prior to a substantial receipt of oil revenues.

The agricultural oil economies, on the other hand, have had to face the problems arising from the country's rural–urban dualism, a high rate of rural–urban migration, the slow development of the agricultural sector, and the associated problem of income distribution. But they are less dependent on food and raw materials imports, and they have the choice of developing their agricultural sectors as part of a broader strategy for the diversification of their economies.[4]

There have been two views on the nature of oil and oil revenues: oil as capital assets, and oil revenues as rent. The two views are not mutually exclusive. If oil revenues are seen as a form of income, economic theory leaves us with little choice but to describe them as rent. But the Ricardian–Marxian concept of differential rent is not easily applicable in this case, because differential rent arises from differences in fertility (or productivity); and, while the marginal farm affords a normal return on labor and capital, it does not afford rent. There is no Middle Eastern oil field that can be described as marginal in this Ricardian sense, for the simple reason that the revenues from "marginal" oil fields in the Middle East (and perhaps elsewhere in OPEC countries) are likely to be significantly higher than the cost of production. Many American oil fields, however, may be in fact marginal in the Ricardian sense; in any case, differential rent theory may explain the differences in earnings of different oil fields within the same country or in average earnings between different countries.

The Smith–Marshal monopoly theory of rent – or, indeed, Marx's theory of absolute rent – may be more applicable to the phenomenon of oil revenues. According to these theories rent arises from the nature and characteristics of the ownership of a resource. There are two basic points: (a) oil resources are ultimately fixed in supply, and are concentrated in certain parts of the world; (b) rather like land under feudalism, and capital in a monopolistic industry, oil resources are subject to monopoly ownership. Therefore, if like land in modern agriculture, the oil resources had been open to the market for purchase and sale, their income would have been a return on capital, for they would then have had a present opportunity cost in terms of alternative assets. It follows that to call oil revenues rent should not necessarily carry any moral implications.[5]

This brings us to the view that oil resources are a collective capital asset, and that oil-exporting countries are living off their capital. In a practical sense this is certainly true, because any finite asset may be either preserved for the future, or be monetized and converted into other assets. Oil resources as such have no *present* opportunity cost because they cannot be sold on the open market – only their product can be. Furthermore, the *future* opportunity costs of these resources would also have to be measured in terms of the future oil revenues. Matters are further complicated because future prices are hard to anticipate and the future time horizon would somehow have to be determined. There is also the problem of determining the social rate of time preference in the case of every oil-exporting economy.

Before proceeding further, it would be useful to settle another

theoretical issue. The terms "oil surplus" or "capital surplus countries" would make sense only insofar as some oil-exporting countries enjoy excess liquidity in foreign exchange or, in other words,
balance-of-payments surpluses over and above their absorptive
capacity. In no other sense could there be a surplus capital anywhere, for, unlike the case of unskilled labor force, the world as a
whole is capital-scarce, and capital has an opportunity cost outside a
country with an abundance of financial resources.[6]

Whether oil revenues are described as a collective rent or as
monetized capital assets, they make their social and economic
impact on the country's economy via the monetary and fiscal decisions of the state. From a purely technical-economic viewpoint
this may seem to be of little importance. Yet, economic theories and
models are based on implicit institutional and behavioral assumptions, and where these assumptions are significantly inapplicable,
theoretical predictions may become invalid. Thus the unique and
unprecedented social and economic freedom and responsibility
which the oil revenues afford to, and demand from, the state could
have decisive consequences for the present and future welfare of the
economy, and for the society of which it is a part. Many years ago
when this point was occasionally being made it was probably too
abstract to attract much attention. But now that we have had a good
deal of experience with problems of development in oil-exporting
countries – and that includes the revolution in Iran – the matter may
have come closer to empirical reality. It is true that the problem of
domestic technological constraints both to the expansion of domestically produced outputs and to the rate of expansion of imports
may by now have been realized and assimilated. Iranian and Saudi
Arabian ports are no longer severely jammed for want of adequate
facilities as they were over the period 1973 to 1976, in part as a result
of better planning, in part because of the expansion of port and
transport capacity, and in part in consequence of a decline in oil
revenues. But the role and responsibility of the state in these
countries is still of paramount importance.[7]

One predictable consequence of the immedite impact of oil revenues in agricultural oil countries such as Iran and Iraq was the lack
of adequate attention to the development of agriculture. Having
virtually no constraint *vis-à-vis* capital and foreign exchange, it was
easy for these countries to experience an unusual degree of independence from their agricultural sectors. But agriculture, and
especially traditional agriculture, is not just an industry but an
integrated social and economic entity in its own right. Where there

is a large agricultural base, it absorbs a large proportion of the population and labor force. Hence rapid urban development without corresponding progress in agricultural countries creates – and has created – serious problems concerning the distribution of income and rural–urban migration. Besides, the physical limitations on imports, and the gestation period for the assimilation of foreign food products proved to be quite serious and had inflationary consequences. Finally, a developed agriculture in the relevant countries could still be an important source of employment, and a source of foreign exchange through its marketed surplus and export surplus. If the aim is economic diversification and the development of alternative export sectors, then agricultural development should readily suggest itself to those oil countries which have the relevant resource endowment.[8]

Because the state is the authority which receives and disburses oil revenues, all the major economic policies and variables – development strategy, public and private consumption, public and private investment, choice of technique, distribution of income, structural change, employment and wage structure, rate of inflation, and so on – have depended on the size and composition of oil revenue disbursement. For example, both in the case of Iran, which is an agricultural oil economy, and in the case of Saudi Arabia, where agriculture has a small share of output and employment, the oil-price hike of 1973–4 quickly led to a high rate of inflation, probably no less than 30% per annum. The sudden increase in the aggregate monetary demand led to demand-pull tendencies, and the domestic economic bottlenecks created a combination of cost-push and structural inflationary pressures.

Another theoretical as well as practical problem concerns the choice of technique. Once again, the direct or indirect attitude of the state largely influences the outcome. The subject is a familiar and controversial one in the literature of development economics. Economic development tends to raise the capital–labor ratio as a result of a structural change in favor of the more capital-intensive products. Furthermore, the choice of producing certain goods would probably constrain the choice of technology used in their production. Beyond these generalities there would normally be *ex ante* factor substitution, but not *ex post*. In other words, producers would face a "putty-clay" situation.

The oil price hike of 1973–4 gave the impression that the oil countries should use highly capital-intensive techniques because of their relative "abundance" of convertible financial capital. In the case of labor-scarce countries such as Saudi Arabia and Kuwait, this may make sense. But countries like Iran have a considerable reservoir of labor in their traditional sectors. Therefore, the choice of a highly capital-intensive technique would create problems for absorbing rural labor, which had been released in consequence of the considerable imbalance in the rural–urban distribution of income. In terms of the Todaro model of rural–urban migration, the fact that the rate of new job creation, though not sufficient, was still high increased the probability of finding a job in the urban sector, thus quickening the pace of labor migration.[9]

A notorious problem of high capital intensity is the scarcity of cooperating domestic inputs, especially skilled and semi-skilled labor. The oil-exporting countries of both types in the region have had to face this problem. The issue has wider social and political dimensions and repercussions, and in the case of Iran it was a contributing factor to the belief that the country was in the hand of Western powers. The Arab oil countries are more fortunate in their ability to draw on the supply of skilled labor force from other Arab countries. But they are not entirely free from actual or potential sociopolitical costs in this respect.

A final point regarding the choice of techniques. It is seldom acknowledged that there are at least two categories of skills in many developing countries: indigenous and acquired. Blacksmiths, cobblers, and so on are skilled with reference to the indigenous technology. Therefore, if the economy chooses a technology which is not greatly dependent on recent technological developments, it would gainfully absorb the pool of indigenous skilled labor. This would reduce costs, extend the effective supply of domestic labor force, and avoid the wastage of traditional skills.

The state's development strategy in Middle Eastern oil-exporting countries has influenced the direction of sectoral development and structural change. The policy everywhere has been expansion and diversification. In Iran and Iraq agriculture has declined fast, but in Saudi Arabia costly efforts have been made to create a small modern agricultural sector. Perhaps it should have been the other way around.[10] Industrial development has taken the form of import substitution, in Iran and Iraq, including a wide range of light industries and consumer durables, as well as heavy and new industrial products. In the non-agricultural countries industrialization has been mainly concentrated in oil refining and petrochemicals as well as the construction-related industries.

Table 3 shows the actual and potential capacity output of organic petrochemicals in the oil-exporting Arab countries. Saudi Arabia is clearly in the lead, partly because of its larger oil revenues, but partly also because of the emphasis it has given to the production and export of petrochemical products. This, in general, is a reasonable strategy for diversification and the development of alternative export industries, and the arguments against it have been rightly put aside.[11]

The trend of structural change has so far been in favor of oil and services. In the case of smaller countries, the oil sector would inevitably dominate in the share of GDP, though not of labor force. Table 4 shows that the share of oil in Kuwait's GDP was 70% (1975–6), and in Iraq's GDP, 63.1% (1975). The oil output as a percentage of Saudi Arabia's GDP was almost 90% (1979–80), but in the case of Iran the oil sector's contribution to GDP was 35.2%. The share of oil in GDP clearly varies over time as a result of the differential rate of growth of this sector relatively to other economic sectors. That is why, for example, the estimated 1984–5 figure for Saudi Arabia is significantly lower than in the previous period.

The more interesting feature of economic structure and structural change in these countries is the high share of services in the GDP. In Kuwait, for example, the GDP share of services is 21.5% compared

Table 3 · Actual and potential capacity output of organic petrochemical products in the oil-exporting Arab countries (1,000 tons, 1980)

	Basic products	Intermediate products	Final products
Algeria	358	40	83
Iraq	135	66	185
Kuwait	780	455	145
Libya	1,200	270	298
Qatar	280	–	210
Saudi Arabia	3,637	1,269	1,204
UAE	450	–	–
OAPEC Joint Companies	–	–	180
Total	6,840	2,100	2,305

Source: Yusif Sayigh, *Arab Oil Policies in the 1970s* (London: Croom Helm, 1983), Table 3.9 (original source: OAPEC, *Secretary General's Annual Report*, 1980).

Table 4 · Percentage distribution of GDP by sectors Iran, Iraq,
Kuwait and Saudi Arabia

	Sectors						
	Agri-culture	Industry	Con-struction	Services	Oil	Total	Oil
Iran							
1967–8	22.6	16.4[a]	5.1	37.4	18.5	100.0 ·	–
1977–8	9.5	14.4[a]	5.3	35.6	35.2	100.0	–
Iraq							
1965	9.0	4.5[a]	2.2	20.3	64.0	100.0	–
1970	8.6	5.1[a]	2.0	21.3	63.0	100.0	–
1975	5.8	5.8[a]	2.3	23.0	63.1	100.0	–
Kuwait							
1970–1	.4	8.0[b]	3.5	20.2	67.9	100.0	–
1975–6	.3	7.3[b]	.9	21.5	70.0	100.0	–
Saudi Arabia							
1979–80[c]	5.8	9.8[a]	21.6	62.8	–	100.0	89.5
1984–5[c]	5.1	18.5[a]	12.6	63.8	–	100.0	64.1

[a] Includes manufacturing, non-oil mining, and public utilities
[b] Includes manufacturing, oil refining, and public utilities
[c] Non-oil GDP; all figures for 1984–5 are estimates.
Sources: Iran: based on *Bank Markazi Iran*, various issues.
    Iraq: United Nations, *National Account Statistics*, 1980.
    Kuwait: M. W. Khouja and P. G. Sadler, *The Economy of Kuwait*
    (London: Macmillan, 1977).
    Saudi Arabia: R. E. Mallakh, *Saudi Arabia: Rush to Development*
    (Baltimore: Johns Hopkins University Press; London: Croom Helm,
    1982).

to 7.3% for industrial activities. Similar observations may be made
not only for Saudi Arabia which has limited agricultural resources,
but also for Iran and Iraq, where a large proportion of the work
force are concentrated in the rural sector. In 1975, the contribution
of Iraq's agriculture to GDP was 5.8%, while its share in the
country's labor force was 43%.[12] Likewise, the GDP share of Iranian agriculture in 1977 was 9.5%, while its share in rural labor
force was 42.5%.[13] These observations have clear implications for
the distribution of income between rural and urban sectors. In Iran,
for example, urban income per capita was at least seven times the
size of rural income per capita in 1976.[14]

There seem to be two trends. First, agriculture declines fast in
agricultural oil countries for the reasons that we have briefly dis-

cussed above. Second, the disbursement of oil revenues and the pattern of consumption they generate tend to promote the service industries. The share of services in the GDP and labor force of many developing countries tends to be larger than is expected at their stage of development. Some developing countries specialize in the export of a few services such as tourism. Many developing countries now produce modern services – banking, insurance, telecommunications, modern medical care and educational facilities, and so on. In the case of oil countries, the relatively high income per capita and the foreign exchange facilities result in a rapid increase in demand for domestic and imported services, especially for those with a high income-elasticity of demand.[15] Table 5 shows the balance of trade in non-factor services in a number of oil-exporting countries. It is evident that they are all in deficit on this account, and that the deficit has been rising fast. Saudi Arabia's deficit (−$24.283 million) is by far the largest in the world for 1980.

Clearly, some of the service imports are due to the increase in

Table 5 · Balance of trade in non-Factor services, selected OPEC countries

| | Current U.S. Dollars | | |
	1970 $ million	1975 $ million	1980 $ million
Algeria	−212	−925	−2,501
Indonesia	−299	−1,212	−3,095
Iran	−382	−2,972	−4,471[a]
Iraq	−0.8	−788	na
Kuwait	na	−329	−1,711
Libya	−399	−1,342	−1,657[b]
Nigeria	−285	−2,395	−3,476
Saudi Arabia	−90	−3,032	−24,283

[a] 1977.
[b] 1979.
Source: Calculated from IMF statistics.

these countries' goods imports, and, where they market their own oil, exports as well. Shipping, insurance, financial and technological services are all part of the service imports. Yet, not all imports are for productive purposes; and at any rate, an economy that has a large domestic service sector as well as a large deficit on the services account must ensure that its production and export sectors develop sufficiently fast to replace the declining oil revenues and exhaustible oil resources in due course.

Average annual rates of growth over the past fifteen years have been high, although the annual rates have varied widely because of the fluctuations in oil revenues. Investment has also increased rapidly, both through government planning and through the private sector. In 1975, gross domestic fixed capital formation in Iraq was more than ten times what it has been in 1960. In the case of Iran, gross fixed investment grew more than eighteenfold between the same dates. Similar patterns apply to all other Middle Eastern oil economies. Much investment has gone into construction which, especially in the case of less developed oil economies, is largely influenced by the rate of infrastructural development. Once again, however, consumption has had a considerable share in this. In Iran, the share of construction in total gross fixed investment (in 1975) was about 60%, less than half of which was spent on residential construction.[16]

The decade of the 1970s was one of consumption boom, even consumerism in Middle Eastern oil countries. In 1979 aggregate consumption for seven Arab oil countries (Algeria, Iraq, Kuwait, Libya, Qatar, Saudi Arabia, UAE) was 43.0% of aggregate GDP; at the same time, it was 120.8% of *non-oil* GDP. In other words, aggregate consumption was $44,681.1 million short of GDP excluding oil.[17] Consumption behavior, once set, is difficult to change, and this may have certain implications for political as well as economic prospects of these countries in times to come, for it shows that the aggregate domestic (i.e., non-oil) saving rate is negative.[18] There are also other problems of a politicoeconomic nature. One is the question of income distribution. It would be difficult to generalize across the board on this question, and in any case the distribution of income and welfare is notoriously difficult to measure in developing countries. But casual observation, partial reports, and a comparison of incomes per worker in various sectors indicate that there is much room for improvement in this respect.[19] The second question is the differences in the standards of living between oil and non-oil economies in the region. For example, in 1979, income per capita in the seven Arab oil countries mentioned above was $4597, whereas in non-oil Arab countries it was $557.[20] It is this kind of comparison that Charles Issawi had in mind when, in 1976, he commented that "the rapid growth of the oil industry [has] a profoundly unequalizing effect" among Arab countries.[21]

Finally, the fact that the propensity to import – or import dependency – of Middle Eastern oil exporters is high is, to some extent, understandable. But given the vicissitudes of the oil sector and the high service imports bill, there may be room for a certain amount of readjustment, especially as regards luxury consumer imports. The total import bill of the same seven Arab oil countries was larger than their non-oil GDP in 1979, almost 90% of their aggregate consumption.[22] These considerations bring us to a brief review of the external impacts of oil and oil revenues.

3. Oil and development: the external impact

The oil price hike of 1973–4 understandably came as a shock to a world that for long had been used to adequate supplies of cheap energy. There was even talk of crisis in the international monetary order, although the origins for this lay in the factors which had led to the dollar devaluations of 1971 and 1973. As Bent Hansen argued at the time, there was also much exaggeration about the size of the existing and future accumulated surpluses by the oil countries.[23] At the time, however, every single oil-exporting country of the Middle East had a greater financial availability than its maximum absorptive capacity, although the size and proportion of the excess liquidity varied considerably from one country to the next.

Apart from international trade and its phenomenal growth between the oil countries and the rest of the world, the major impact of these countries on the region and elsewhere was felt in two important ways: the import of migrant workers by Middle Eastern oil countries, and the export of capital from them.

All of these countries needed to import skilled manpower, and several had a shortage of unskilled workers as well. The share of guest workers in Saudi Arabia's labor force alone was more than 41% of its total labor force in 1975, and estimates show that this would be appreciably more in 1985. Table 6 shows that in 1975, more than 1.6 million guest workers were distributed among the main labor-importing countries of the Middle East, and that the figure is likely to rise to more than 3.5 million in 1985. A migration of this magnitude has important social and economic implications both for host countries and for the countries from which most migrant workers come. Saudi Arabia has by far the largest share of the total number of migrant workers, followed by Libya, UAE, and the others. A large proportion of the migrant workers are from non-oil Arab countries taken together, but India and Pakistan also have high shares in the total.

Many guest workers in Arab oil economies come from non-oil Arab countries. There are both costs and benefits in this. The common ethnic origin and language of hosts and guests result in greater efficiency and integrability of the migrant workers. On the other hand, problems may arise from divisions of loyalty, or the ease with which Arab migrants may be able to grow roots in their host countries.

Table 6 · Distribution of migrant workers in the main labor-importing countries of the Middle East

	1975		1985 (estimated)	
	Numbers (1,000)	% of Total	Numbers (1,000)	% of Total
Bahrain	29.1	1.8	81.4	2.3
Kuwait	210.6	13.1	273.4	7.7
Libya	280.4	17.5	719.3	20.3
Oman	103.2	6.5	107.0	3.0
Qatar	61.3	3.8	116.7	3.3
Saudi Arabia	668.4	41.7	1,679.9	47.3
UAE	247.8	15.6	570.7	16.1
Total	1,600.8	100.0	3,548.4	100.0

Source: I. Serageldin, et al., *Manpower and International Labor Migration in the Middle East and North Africa* (New York: Published for the World Bank by Oxford University Press, 1983), Table 1.1.

Table 7 shows the distribution of guest workers according to the country of origin. Egypt supplied 350,000 workers in 1975, and the number is estimated to rise to more than 700,000 in 1985. Another Arab country, North Yemen, has contributed 330,000, likely to rise to 400,000 in 1985. Among the non-Arab countries, the countries of the Indian subcontinent have a large share of the total, and it is likely that a good number of workers from this region are skilled. The degree of interdependence in the export of labor in the region is clearly high, and given the human aspects of the case, its future management would require a considerable amount of delicacy.

Table 8 refers to another important aspect of the same subject. The exporting of workers' results in two immediate benefits to the exporting country: reduction in domestic unemployment, and growth of foreign exchange earnings. To the extent that this results

Table 7 · Labour exporters to the main importing countries

Labour exporting countries	1975		1985	
	Number (1,000)	% of Total	Number (1,000)	% of Total
Arab countries				
Egypt	353.3	22.1	711.5	20.1
Iran	69.9	4.4	115.6	3.3
Iraq	18.7	1.2	12.4	0.3
Jordan	139.0	8.7	257.4	7.2
Lebanon	28.9	1.8	70.4	2.0
Morocco	2.2	0.1	12.5	0.4
Oman	30.8	1.9	46.0	1.3
Sudan	26.0	1.6	38.1	2.5
Syria	38.1	2.4	96.1	2.7
Tunisia	29.3	1.8	62.8	1.8
Yemen (A.R.)	328.5	20.5	400.8	11.3
Yemen (P.D.R.)	45.8	2.9	84.7	2.4
Other				
India	141.9	8.9	360.7	10.2
Pakistan	205.7	12.8	541.3	15.2
East Asia	20.5	1.3	370.5	10.4
Rest of the world	122.2	7.6	317.6	8.9
Total	1,600.8	100.0	3,498.4	100.0

Source: I. Serageldin, et al., *Manpower and International Labor Migration in the Middle East and North Africa* (New York: Published for the World Bank by Oxford University Press, 1983), Table 1.2.

Table 8 · Workers' remittances as a percentage of merchandise exports, selected countries

	1967	1973	1978–9
Egypt	4.4	11.7	88.8
Jordan	58.8	60.8	175.4
Morocco	12.4[a]	27.4	51.5
Sudan	0.5	1.2	12.2
Syria	3.2	10.4	8.8
Tunisia	13.3	23.8	24.6
Yemen (A.R.)	–	1,373.1	7,091.3
Yemen (P.D.R.)	83.7	1,340.0	5,638.0

[a] 1968

Sources: based on A. Swamy, *International Migrant Workers' Remittances: Issues and Prospects*, World Bank Staff Working Paper no. 48(1981), Table 3.

in a shortage of skilled manpower at home, there may be a cost involved, although as a rule the exporting countries suffer from graduate unemployment as well. Workers' remittances, however, have become an important source of factor service earnings for a few developing countries, many of which are located in the region. Table 8 shows that North Yemen's earnings from this service, in 1973, was 13 times, and in 1978–9, 70 times, its merchandise exports. Similar figures are found for South Yemen. In the case of Jordan, the remittance/merchandise-export ratio for 1978–9 is 175%. But perhaps it is even more impressive that for Egypt the figure is nearly 89%.The ratio is an index of interdependence, and in a simple way it shows how, in spite of appearances, the fortunes of both oil and non-oil countries of the region have become intertwined.

The second important impact of the rise in oil prices and revenues has been on the size and distribution of foreign aid and investment by the oil-exporting countries. In general, the oil countries, and especially the large surplus countries of the Middle East, faced a number of choices regarding the deployment of these surpluses. Investment in the West seemed less risky, although it was probably less rewarding. Indeed, the negative real rate of interest in the West for much of the 1970s resulted in the erosion of the real value of these assets over a number of years. Furthermore, there was a greater tendency to place the funds in liquid assets rather than invest in industrial property and other productive activities.

In practice, the surpluses were deployed both in developed and in developing countries, in real and in monetary assets as well as in grants and concessionary loans to other less developed countries. Just after the oil price increases of 1973 and 1979, the proportion of the oil-exporting countries' assets held in the form of bank deposits was 57% and 51%, respectively. In addition, large purchases were made on short-term government paper, especially U.S. treasury bills. There has been a reluctance to invest heavily in other assets, though the proportion of the assets held in equity, property, and the like, has increased from 13% in 1974 to 29% in 1983.[24] Investment by smaller countries in bigger countries is probably no less risky than the other way around, and the seizure of Iranian assets by the U.S. government for apparently political reasons did not add much to confidence in the Middle East.

Table 9 shows the identified deployment of OPEC funds over the period 1974–83. The United States has had the largest share of the cumulative inflow (22.7%), followed by the United Kingdom

Table 9 · Identified deployment of OPEC funds 1974–83

1974–83	Flow of funds		Levels ($ billion)		
	($ billions)	% of total	1973	1979	1983
United States	83.3	22.7	3.5	47.8	85.9
United Kingdom	55.9	15.3	7.3	57.5	83.1
Germany	24.3	6.6	–	15.6	21.6
Other industrialized countries	113.4	30.9	0.6	80.1	117.2
IMF and World Bank	18.6	5.1	2.2	10.5	20.8
Bank credit to non-banks	12.3	3.4	–	6.0	13.0
Developing countries	58.3	16.0	–	39.7	58.3
Total	366.1	100.0			

Source: based on *Bank of England Quarterly Bulletin* (March 1985).

(15.3%). In all, more than 75% of the funds have been deployed in industrial countries. The cumulative flow to the developing countries was 16% of the total, but its absolute level, $58.5 billion, was by no means a derisory sum. By any account, the OPEC foreign aid – most of it from the Middle East – has been quite generous, although it could have been even higher.

A comparison of selected aid donors in Table 10 shows that Saudi Arabian aid in 1981 was marginally less than that of the United

Table 10 · Foreign aid comparison: selected donors

	Share in total aid (%)		Aid as a percentage of GNP	
	1975	1981	1975	1981
United States	21.7	16.1	0.3	0.2
Saudi Arabia	14.4	15.8	7.7	4.7
France	10.9	11.7	0.6	0.7
West Germany	8.8	8.9	0.4	0.5
Japan	6.0	8.9	0.2	0.3
United Kingdom	4.7	6.1	0.4	0.4
UAE	5.5	2.2	11.7	2.9
Kuwait	4.9	1.9	7.4	2.0

Source: based on UNCTAD, *Trade and Development Report*, 1983, Table 9, p. 65

Table 11 · Selected developing countries:[a] net receipts of foreign
aid from OPEC as a percentage of total foreign aid receipts,
1979–81

	1979	1980	1981
Oman	98.1	96.6	97.6
Bahrain	96.8	97.8	97.4
Jordan	87.6	82.0	83.8
Syria	91.9	93.5	82.6
Lebanon	64.9	83.7	82.5
Yemen	64.5	71.5	68.1
Morocco	63.9	62.5	50.8
Sudan	53.3	30.0	29.0
Turkey	91.2	27.4	26.1
Somalia	43.7	33.4	14.6
Pakistan	4.6	32.0	1.6
Egypt[b]	14.4	0.9	–
India[b]	1.7	4.6	–

[a] Countries whose receipts of OPEC bilateral ODA exceeded $100 million in any
one of the years covered.
[b] Debt repayments exceed gross receipts in 1981.
Source: UNCTAD, *Trade and Development Report*, 1983, Table 7, p. 62.

States, and larger than all other major aid donors. Furthermore, in
terms of the percentage share of the GNP, Saudi Arabian aid was by
far the largest of the whole group. The average annual flow of aid
from Saudi Arabia over the period 1973–81 was $3,716 million, 60%
of the total for seven oil-exporting countries of the Middle East. It
was followed by UAE and Kuwait, which also had significantly
large shares of the total.

The question of foreign aid, like that of migrant workers and their
remittances has another aspect to it, namely, the aid recipients.
Much aid from the Middle Eastern oil countries has flowed to other
countries in the region, though the countries outside the region
have not been entirely excluded. Table 11 shows that in some cases
(e.g., Oman) the net receipt of OPEC aid has been almost as much
as aid flowing from the rest of the world. In fact, the proportion of
OPEC aid has been high in many cases (compare Jordan, Syria,
Lebanon, Yemen, and Morocco). Once again, this reveals the
degree to which oil revenues have spilled over to the neighboring
countries. The recent tendency for the decline of oil revenues is
bound to have an effect on the size and terms of foreign aid and

Table 12 · Combined current account of the oil-exporting
countries, 1973–1983 ($ billions)

Year	Exports			Imports	Balance of trade	Invisible balance	Current balance
	Energy	Other	Total				
1973	37	4	41	22	19	−13	6
1974	116	57	173	39	84	−17	67
1975	110	6	116	59	57	−25	32
1976	130	8	138	73	65	−29	36
1977	146	9	155	89	66	−41	25
1978	141	10	151	106	45	−48	−3
1979	208	13	221	107	114	−55	59
1980	298	15	313	136	177	−67	110
1981	273	13	286	157	129	−80	49
1982	210	13	223	156	67	−82	−15
1983	182	15	197	136	61	−76	−15

Source: based on *Bank of England Quarterly Bulletin* (March 1985).

grant from Middle Eastern oil-exporting countries. In this regard, the figures in Table 11 give the observer food for thought.

Table 12 shows that for the first time since 1982 the combined current account balance of the oil-exporting countries is in deficit. Not surprisingly, countries with a higher rate of crude exports at lower absorptive capacity are in a better position than the others. But even in their case, financial availability has been drastically reduced, and the ability to export capital correspondingly constrained. Saudi Arabia, for example, is now exporting oil at an estimated rate of a quarter of its exports in 1979–80, and at a lower nominal as well as real price. The implications of this trend for the domestic and external effects of oil revenues, and perhaps for the future of OPEC as well, should not be underrated.

NOTES

1 See H. Katouzian, *The Political Economy of Modern Iran* (London, Macmillan, & New York, New York University Press: 1981), ch. 7, Tables 9.2 and 9.3. See further, M. Fateh, *Panjah Sal Naft-i Iran* (Tehran, 1956); E. Abrahamian, *Iran between Two Revolutions* (Princeton, N. J.: Princeton University Press, 1982); and Nikki R. Keddie, *Roots of Revolution* (New Haven: Yale University Press, 1981).

2 See further, F. J. Al-Chalabi, *OPEC and the International Oil Industry: A Changing Structure* (New York: Oxford University Press, 1980); Yusif Sayigh, *Arab Oil Policies in the 1970s* (London: Croom Helm, 1980); I. Seymour, *OPEC; An Instrument of Change* (New York: St. Martin's Press, 1980); D. Venouss, C. K. Walter, and A. F. Thompson, "OPEC's Goal and Strategies," *International Journal of Middle East Studies*, 16 (May 1984), 199–206; and H. Beblawi, *The Arab Gulf Economy in a Turbulent Age* (London: Croom Helm, 1984), ch. 1.

3 For an excellent summary report of events leading up to the 1985 price decrease, see Robert Mabro, "Petroleum Commentary," *Arab Gulf Journal*, 5, no. 1 (April 1985), 3–7.

4 See further, H. Katouzian, "The Political Economy of Oil Exporting Countries," *Mediterranean Peoples*, no. 8 (September 1979), 3–22, and idem, *The Political Economy of Modern Iran*, ch. 12.

5 See further, H. Mahdavi, "Rentier States," in Michael Cook, ed., *Studies in the Economic History of the Middle East* (London: Oxford University Press, 1970); Thomas Staufer, "The Dynamics of Petroleum Dependency: Growth in a Rentier State," *Finance and Industry*, no. 2 (1981), 7–28; and idem, *The Political Economy of Modern Iran*.

6 Katouzian, "The Political Economy of Oil Exporting Countries" and idem, *The Political Economy of Modern Iran*

7 On the political economy of the state in the oil-exporting countries, see Katouzian references in note 6, above.

8 On the role of agriculture in an oil-exporting country, see H. Katouzian, "The Agrarian Question in Iran," in A. K. Ghose, ed., *Agrarian Reform in Contemporary Developing Countries* (London: Croom Helm, 1983).

9 For Todaro's migration model, see Michael Todaro, *Economic Development in the Third World* (3rd ed.; New York: Longman, 1985), and idem, "Income Expectations, Rural–Urban Migration, and Employment in Africa," *International Labour Review*, 104 (July–December 1971), 387–413. For the problem of rural–urban migration in Iran, see Katouzian, "The Agrarian Question in Iran" and idem, *The Political Economy of Modern Iran*. In the 1970s the rate of population growth in Iran was 2.9%, and the rate of rural–urban migration was as high as 1.7%. The urban income per capita was at least seven times, and probably ten times that of average increases in the rural areas; see further below.

10 Much of the costs are incurred in the production of fresh water supplies through desalinization of sea water as well as the exploitation of underground water reservoirs. See, for example, R. El Mallakh, *Saudi Arabia: Rush to Development* (Baltimore: Johns Hopkins University Press, & London: Croom Helm, 1982).

11 For a good summary evaluation of the arguments for and against the development of petrochemical industries in Saudi Arabia and other Middle Eastern oil countries, see Y. A. Stournaras, "Is the Industrial-

ization of the Arab Gulf a Rational Policy?" *Arab Gulf Journal*, 5, no. 1 (April 1985), 21–7. See further, H. G. Hambleton, "The Saudi Petrochemical Industry," in R. El-Mallakh and D. H. El-Mallakh, eds., *Saudi Arabia: Energy, Development Planning and Industrialization* (Lexington, Mass.: Lexington Books, 1982).

12 See I. A. Hammadi, *Economic Growth and Structural Change in the Iraqi Economy* (Ann Arbor: University Microfilms International, 1981).

13 Katouzian, *The Political Economy of Modern Iran*, ch. 14.

14 See H. Katouzian, "Oil *versus* Agriculture: A Case of Dual Resource Depletion in Iran," *Journal of Peasant Studies*, 5 (April 1978), 347–69.

15 See further, H. Katouzian, "The Development of the Service Sector: A New Approach," *Oxford Economic Papers*, Series 2, 22 (November 1970), 262–82; also idem, "Oil *versus* Agriculture" and idem, *The Political Economy of Modern Iran*.

16 For figures concerning gross fixed domestic capital formation and its subdivisions, see United Nations, *National Accounts Statistics*, 1980.

17 These figures are based on the data in Sayigh, *Arab Oil Policies in the 1970s*, Tables 4.2 and 4.3.

18 This has also been true in Iran in the periods 1962–78. See Katouzian, *The Political Economy of Modern Iran*, Table 13.6.

19 See, for example, ibid., Tables 13.4 and 13.10–13.13.

20 See Sayigh, *Arab Oil Policies in the 1970s*.

21 See Charles Issawi's article, "The Economy of the Middle East and North Africa: An Overview," in A. L. Udovitch, ed., *The Middle East: Oil, Conflict and Hope* (Lexington, Mass.: Lexington Books, 1976).

22 See Sayigh, *Arab Oil Policies in the 1970s*.

23 See Bent Hansen, "The Accumulation of Financial Capital by the Middle East Oil Exporters," in A. L. Udovitch, ed., *The Middle East: Oil, Conflict and Hope*.

24 See further, *Bank of England Quarterly Bulletin* (March 1985).

4 · Capital and lopsided development in Egypt under British occupation

BENT HANSEN

University of California, Berkeley

In a seminal paper Charles Issawi characterized economic development in Egypt until the 1950s as "lopsided."[1] The characterization refers to the investment policy, initiated by Mohammed Ali, continued by Ismail, and further pursued and completed by the British, aiming at increasing cotton cultivation and cotton export. For the British it became a matter of increasing foreign as well as public revenues to render the service payments on Egypt's public debt feasible and palatable to the Egyptian population. It can be argued that, ignoring diversification,[2] this was a high-risk policy from the point of view of both the Egyptian population and the foreign owners of the public debt. It can be argued, moreover, that supplying Egyptian high-quality cotton along a downward sloping foreign demand curve, thus sacrificing Egypt's terms of trade,[3] may have been self-defeating from a debt-service point of view, harmful to the Egyptian population at large, and beneficial only to "Lancashire," that is, to the world consumers.

Were the public, cotton-oriented investments a mistake? Should the country have embarked upon industrialization alongside agricultural development? If the answer is "Yes," from where should the necessary capital come? And how should capital be induced to go into industry? These are the problems I propose to discuss. I cannot do that in a meaningful way, however, without surveying first capital inflows and savings-investment patterns in Egypt during the crucial years before World War I.

Capital accumulation, 1884–1913

We have reliable information about capital accumulation by *central government* for the period 1884–1913. The data are presented in Table 1. Public savings (the budget surplus) and sales of property

Table 1 · Capital flow account, central government, 1884–1913, cumulated

Available	LE Million	Use	LE Million
Public saving	44	Irrigation and drainage	19
Sales of property	23	Infrastructure	22
		Increased cash holdings	3
		Net lending (residual)	23
Total	67	Total	67

Source: Bent Hansen, "Saving and Investments, Flow of Funds, Egypt, 1884–1913," Working Paper no 135, Department of Economics, University of California, Berkeley (October 1979), pp. 20–4, Table 3. Infrastructure includes transportation.

(land) provided the government with LE 67 million, which were used for net investments (not including, maintenance and repair): in irrigation and drainage, 19 million; infrastructure, 22 million; and net lending, 23 million, apart from a small amount held as cash. Net lending went mainly to repayment of public debt abroad, 14 million; and credits related to sales of property, 9 million. The LE 19 million invested by the public sector in the hydraulic system between 1882 and 1914 was a relatively modest amount compared with the total inflow of capital of LE 75 million during the same period. Considering also domestic savings, it would appear that private and public investments outside the hydraulic system together must have exceeded the latter by a factor of perhaps 3 to 4. It is true that private capital inflow, and private saving and investment were not the outcome of deliberate government policies. Yet, any evaluation of the public hydraulic investments must consider other investments and their sources of financing.

For the years 1903–13 detailed accounts may be established for both the government and the private sector (the latter with a breakdown on joint-stock companies and the non-incorporated private sector, not included here).[4] These were the years when private foreign capital flooded the country. Table 2 specifies capital flow accounts for central government, private sector, and Egypt, consolidated. The figures should be interpreted as net of depreciation and replacement and are shown as annual averages. This has the advantage that they may also (approximately) be read as

Table 2 · Capital flow accounts, Egypt: 1903–1913 (Annual averages, LE million, appr. = % of GNP)

Available	LE Million	Use	LE Million
I. Central Government[a]			
Public Saving	2.3	Fixed investment, total	2.6
Sale of Property	1.4	Irrigation & drainage 1.1	
Fiduciary coins, issue	0.1	Infrastructure, other 1.4	
		Increased cash holding	0.2
		Repayment of foreign debt, net	0.6
		Lending to private sector, net	0.5
Total	3.9	Total	3.9
II. Private Sector[b]			
Private saving, total	2.7	Direct foreign investment	0.4
Companies	0.9	Fixed investment, total	4.0
Personal	1.8	Agriculture 1.3	
Foreign capital inflow, net	5.8	Industry 0.8[e]	
Direct investment	0.4	Infrastructure 0.8	
Financial investment	6.2	Urban real estate 1.1	
of which: waste[c]	−0.8	Inventories, etc.[d]	1.5
Borrowing from central		Purchase of land from government	1.4
government, net	0.5	Species	1.7
Subtotal	9.0	Subtotal	9.0
Capital gains, total	20.9	Capital gains, total	20.9
Agricultural land	16.6	Agricultural land 16.6	
Urban real estate	2.5	Urban real estate 2.5	
Crops, etc.	1.8	Crops, etc. 1.8	
Total	29.9	Total	29.9
III. Egypt, Consolidated Account			
Domestic saving, total	5.0	Fixed investments, total	6.5
Public	2.3	Agriculture, public 1.1	
Private	2.7	Agriculture, private 1.3	
Direct foreign investment	0.4	Industry 0.8	
Net sale of claims on Egypt	4.9	Infrastructure, public 1.4	
		Infrastructure, private 0.8	
		Urban real estate 1.1	
		Inventories, etc.	1.5
		Direct foreign investment	0.4
		Species	1.9
Total	10.3	Total	10.3

[a] Including Caisse de la dette, State domains, Daira sanieh.
[b] Not including Suez Canal Company
[c] Capital lost in liquidated companies
[d] Including crops, growing or stored
[e] Including hotels
Source: Bent Hansen, "Saving and Investments, Flow of Funds, Egypt, 1884–1913," Working Paper no. 135, Department of Economics, University of California, Berkeley, (October 1979). Details do not always add up to totals because of roundings.

per cents of national income, average national income being of the order LE 100 million during the period 1903–13. Needless to say, the estimates behind Table 2 are at many points crude and uncertain; methods of estimation, with possible errors and omissions, are discussed in the basic source of the table. For the private sector, crude estimates of capital gains are shown in a special self-balancing subaccount. Capital gains on real assets in the country are not, of course, a source of financing at the national level; they are bottled up where they occur. Capital gains are crucial, nonetheless, for understanding the composition of capital accumulation during this period; capital gains induce portfolio restructuring and serve as collateral for mortgage and other loans, necessary for such restructuring. Thus there is little doubt that large amounts of foreign capital, via mortgage loans in agricultural land, financed investments made by residents in equity (in companies and urban real estate), purchases of land from the government, and hoarding of species. Capital gains for Egypt through the decline of the value of foreign debt in terms of exports or imports are not included. Important though these were, quantitatively they have little bearing on the present discussion.[5]

Total net investments seem to have been running at a level of 10% of national income, sufficient perhaps, considering the nature of the investments, for generating a growth rate of about 3%. The rate of increase of population was 1.2%. At this rate of growth, per capita income at the outbreak of World War II should have been about double that at the turn of the century. That did not happen; per capita income was probably lower in 1939 than in 1900.

Domestic savings ran at a level of 5% of national income.[6] Thus about half the investments were financed from abroad. With no foreign capital initially and a very small foreign investment flow the whole increase in the national product, caused by the foreign capital inflow, would theoretically accrue to the foreign investor. In the present case, however, the initial stock of foreign capital in the private sector was substantial, the new inflow was very large, and the average rate of profits fell from about 9.5% to about 5.9% during the decade before World War I.[7] Foreign capital did operate behind a protective barrier, but the level of protection was low and it does not seem that capital-intensive production was particularly protected. There is no reason for believing, thus, that return of foreign capital should have skimmed off the whole increase in the domestic product related to the capital inflow. Hence, the rate of growth of national income per capita may have increased as a result of foreign financing, assuming that investment would have been correspondingly lower without foreign financing. If per capita income did not increase from 1900 to 1939 – and most probably it did not – we have to look for other explanations. The most likely explanation is a decline in total factor productivity in agriculture.[8] In addition, terms of trade were adverse during most of the interwar period.

For the period 1903–13, investments were remarkably diversified. Only about one tenth of total net investments, that is about one percent of national income went into the public hydraulic system. About one-quarter went into production of traded goods and services; here I include private investments in agriculture, industry and hotels, and direct foreign investments. About one-third went into non-traded services (infrastructure other than hydraulics, and urban real estate). The remaining one third went into inventories and species (gold). Investments in fixed capital in industry were very low, however, and gold hoarding remarkably high, 0.8% against 1.9% of national income, respectively.

Accusations of lopsided development have mainly concentrated upon comparisons between hydraulic and industrial investments. I shall discuss the composition of investments more generally. Given the total, was the composition of investments irrational from a national point of view? If so, what was the reason? Could and should alternative investment policies have been followed? In discussing these problems we have to face the fact that not only was the country occupied by the British, who interfered heavily into Egyptian affairs, but also that the country was tied up in the straightjacket of the Capitulatory Treaties which acted as a constraint also upon the British. It is true that the Anglo-French Agreement of 1904 freed the British considerably by removing the budgetary controls of the Caisse; yet, until the 1930s the capitulations continued to severely limit the freedom of action of the rulers of Egypt, whoever they were.

In discussing hypothetical policy alternatives we are, of course, at liberty to choose our assumptions about the degree of independency and autonomy as we see fit. I have chosen in this paper to discuss capital accumulation with the Capitulary Treaties considered a fact of life. This appears to me to be the only way of pinpointing the responsibilities of the British, who were in no position to ignore, even less to abrogate, the capitulations should they have desired to do so. The main implications for our problem are that without consent from the Powers:

1. Tariffs could not be increased over and above 8% *ad valorem* for imports (4% for coal, charcoal, mazout, fire wood, construction timber, live animals, and meat, with special higher rates for tobacco) and 1% for exports;

2. New direct taxes could not be imposed upon foreigners, and hence were not politically acceptable to Egyptians, over and above the existing land and urban property taxes, the rates of which could not be increased either without approval of the Powers.[9] The prohibition did not apply to excises and taxes on the products of local industry.[10]

This would obviously face any government with severe constraints on the creation of incentives for, and domestic financing of, industrialization through budgetary measures.

In defense of the British hydraulic investments

Despite the criticism raised against the British development policy as being "lopsided" and the British being "obsessed" with hydraulic investments, I do not think that anybody would seriously argue that these investments should not have been made, or should not have been made at the time they actually were made.[11] Generally, to argue like that would simply mean denying the viability of "green revolution" as a development policy. More specifically:

1. The British, as a matter of fact, only put the final touches upon hydraulic works that had been initiated under Mohammed Ali and his followers; the British continued to pursue the same investment policy. The aim was to introduce perennial irrigation with a two-crop system in Delta and Valley. Cost-benefit analysis of these investments has never been made, to the best of my knowledge; an attempt would be worthwhile. Available information indicates very high profitability, private as well as social. The value of each annual cotton crop sufficed for paying off the whole stock of capital (Table 3). By and large this remained true until the end of the 1920s.

Cotton was not the only benefit from the hydraulic system and capital was not the only cost factor. Some crops were squeezed out by cotton and labor input in agriculture must have increased. Nonetheless, it seems beyond reasonable doubt that these were socially highly profitable investments and, most probably, socially the best use that possibly could be made out of this capital at that time. With the Great Depression and the huge hydraulic investments in the 1930s conditions changed dramatically; but then the responsibility for the economy had already passed to the Egyptian government.

Table 3 · Hydraulic capital and cotton crop, 1882–1937 (LE million at current prices)

Year	(1) Stock of capital, irrigation, and drainage	(2) Value of cotton crop
1882	9.8	(9.0)
1892	10.6	13.3
1902	13.9	20.2
1912	30.3	31.6
1928	61.9	47.7
1937	68.3	27.2

Sources, col. (1): Sadmir Radwan, "Capital Formation in Egyptian Industry and Agriculture, 1882–1967," Thesis, University of London, SOAS (September 1973), Table 2.1
col. (2): For 1882–1912, E. R. G. Owen, *Cotton and the Egyptian Economy, 1820–1914: A Study in Trade and Development* (Oxford: Clarendon Press, 1969), Table 37; for 1928 and 1937, R. L. Tignor, *Private Enterprise and Economic Change in Egypt, 1918–1952* (Princeton, N.J.: Princeton University Press), Table 4.2.

2. It is well known that the design of the hydraulic system turned out to be inadequate and that profitability could have been even higher had designs been adequate.[12] Critical voices were raised already in the 1890s before the decline in yields was a matter of fact.[13] Major Brown's defense of the designs indicates that tight budgets, until 1904 imposed by the Caisse de la dette, may have tempted the British administration to take design risks that, with the wisdom of hindsight, it clearly should not have taken;[14] but, basically, this appears to have been an honest difference of opinion amongst highly skillful engineers where the critics turned out to be right. That the damage done was not ultimately repaired until the late 1930s, although the remedies were understood and partly implemented before World War I, was related to the shortages of supplies and tight budgets during World War I and its aftermath. Had Egypt not been geared to the British war efforts, yields might have been restored earlier. Seventy-five years later the Nasser government was to repeat the British mistake. Alongside the construction of the Aswan High Dam, it completely neglected the need for additional drainage facilities despite warnings from both the Soviet engineers, who designed the High Dam, and the local experts in the Ministries of Agriculture and Irrigation, where the

experience of the British was not forgotten. This fact should caution modern critics against blaming the British for what in their case essentially was a matter of incomplete knowledge and experience.

3. Egyptian agriculture was not tied mechanically to cotton via the hydraulic system. Agriculture could be switched away from cotton towards other crops almost overnight, and the number of alternative crops that could be grown increased greatly with the new hydraulic system. In that sense Egyptian agriculture, and hence the Egyptian economy, potentially became much more diversified as a consequence of the hydraulic investments. These were initiated as an export promoting device. Cotton became the key crop simply because it remained the most profitable crop even at relatively low cotton prices and even considering the higher risk involved by the relative volatility of cotton prices; otherwise cotton would not have been grown by private growers. Nobody forced the big landlords into growing cotton. Had they preferred to grow two food crops rather than one cotton crop with a one-cut clover crop every second or third year, the water rotation in the canals would surely have been adjusted accordingly. Egypt would then have become a grain and flour exporter as was the case before the mid-nineties, but this would have been a matter of relative agricultural prices. The composition of agricultural output was not technically predetermined by the investments in the hydraulic system.

4. A few words are in order about the argument that the continued expansion of cotton cultivation was harmful of the terms of trade of Egypt.[15] To what extent this economic mechanism (fully understood after World War I when Egypt did make attempts to limit the supply of Egyptian cotton to the world market) really operated against Egypt, would entirely depend upon the elasticity of foreign demand for Egyptian cotton. Unfortunately, the long-term elasticity of foreign demand at that time is not known. Quite a few econometric estimates of this elasticity have been made. The results generally point to a relatively low elasticity of demand, not much higher than unity. All the estimates, however, suffer seriously from specification errors. They mostly do not distinguish between short- and long-term demand. They do not explicitly model speculation, which may tend to make the elasticity very high in the short term, or substitution (in textile production and consumption) with supply response in other countries, all of which tend to make the elasticity high also in the long run. I myself have made attempts to model and estimate the demand for Egyptian cotton.[16] After much work I now feel convinced that available data do not suffice for

estimating a demand function with satisfactory specifications. We simply do not know what the long-term elasticity of demand was; most probably we shall never know. With Ahmed Abdel Wahab's famous *memorandum* on a cotton policy in 1930, arguing that Egypt's crop was too small for influencing world market prices (meaning, apparently, that the elasticity of demand was very high) Egypt gave up attempts to pursue supply policies. Abdel Wahab's policy has been interpreted as being pro-British and harmful to Egypt. Whatever his personal intentions were, he may have been right – we just cannot know.[17]

5. A final point, of importance for, among other things, the need for industrialization, is that the hydraulic investments and the change towards the two-crop system with cotton the key-crop appear to have been strongly land-saving and labor-demanding. Comparisons of real agricultural wages, in terms of agricultural output, and agricultural output per unit of labor indicate a strong increase in marginal as compared with average productivity of labor. For land exactly the opposite happened: Real rental of land fell strongly as compared with output per acre. Seen against the background of a Cobb-Douglass production function this would indicate a bias in technological change in favor of labor and against land.[18] As a result, not only did functional income distribution in agriculture shift strongly in favor of labor from 1900 (perhaps even earlier) to 1939, agriculture was also able to absorb a large increase in the labor force on an almost unchanged cultivated area without a decline in agricultural real wages and despite a decline in total factor productivity in Egyptian agriculture. This must have alleviated the labor market situation and the urgency of industrialization.

Investments in infrastructure and urban real estate

More than half the public fixed investments outside the hydraulic system went into infrastructure such as railways, roads, ports, and so on. Thanks to the budgetary stringencies imposed by the Caisse de la dette, public transportation, in particular the railways, were in a poor shape at the time of the Anglo-French Agreement of 1904. The relatively high level of investments in public infrastructure outside the hydraulic system thereafter was probably justified from any point of view.

Private infrastructure investments were about two thirds of those in the public sector. A substantial part of the investments were preparations for residential building activity; an important example is the Heliopolis–Oasis Company, which during these years constructed the Heliopolis–Cairo metro and laid out roads and sewers for the new suburb. These private investments proved to be highly profitable in the long run, and it would be difficult to argue against them on social grounds unless considerations of income and wealth distribution are brought into the picture. Private infrastructure investments during this period served to a considerable extent to satisfy demand from the high-income and wealth brackets.

Much the same can be said about private investments in urban real estate. Demand for modern housing increased strongly during the 1890s and in the first years of the twentieth century because of a large inflow of foreigners, an increase in the number of rural absentee landlords, and high urban profits accompanying the increase in cotton prices from 1897 to 1907. Mortgage loans in agricultural land were probably a major source of financing. The residential building boom that broke down in 1908 was interrelated, however, with the stock market bubble that so much excited public opinion at the time and later economic historians, and which came to an end in June 1907 with the collapse of Casa di Sconto and some other banking institutions. This interrelationship is difficult to disentangle. Agricultural land prices apparently rose in proportion to agricultural prices and the decline in domestic interest rates but speculation in agricultural land prices was not pronounced.[19] Speculation was closely geared to urban land and property values, reflected in stock market prices for companies operating in urban property. The speculation in urban land values was triggered by the urban building boom. To judge from the import of building materials it started in the 1890s as explained above.[20] Stock market speculation appears to have peaked in 1905 and may have played a role in creating demand for modern housing. Yet, I do not think that the collapse of the speculative bubble was the cause of the collapse of the building boom. Already in early June 1907, before the Casa di Sconto crisis, oversupply of housing was predicted for 1908, simply as a consequence of the volume of apartments under construction.[21] Personally, I look at the residential building boom from the 1890s through the recession in 1908 and 1919, with recovery in 1911–12 and even more so after World War I, as a typical local Kuznets-cycle, parallel to but independent of the simultaneous Kuznets-cycle in England. The stock market bubble was an accompanying "surface" phenomenon. It is important to emphasize that no capital was "absorbed" by or disappeared into stock market speculation; at most the speculative activities may have tightened the credit market. The problem is whether the building boom and its collapse implied waste of capital that could have been used for better purposes. Overbuilding did take place, and vacancies in the housing market were widespread from 1908 to 1911. Demand for housing, however, caught up again at a high level of rents. If there was waste of capital here, it was the kind of waste that is involved by the business cycles of the capitalist system everywhere and at all times.

Investments in infrastructure and urban real estate absorbed about one third of all capital invested in Egypt from 1903 to 1913. They all lead to production of non-traded services, but this, of course, does not mean that these investments in themselves should have been inferior to, say, investments in industry.

Inventories

Planners as well as historians have a remarkable ability to overlook the need for investments in inventories. No economy can function without inventories and a growing economy must use some capital for inventory investments. In the present case, about one third of the estimated inventory investments were growing crops, either in the fields or in storage. Growing crops need financing; indeed, it is the need for financing crops that forces poor peasants to go to the moneylender. Inventories may be related to exports, imports, import substitutes, or non-tradeable commodities. In any case, inventories are productive. While excessive inventories may have been cumulated during the hectic years of the 1904–6 boom (the item "waste," equal to LE 0.8 million in Table 2 was probably mainly related to inventories), there is little to indicate that for the period 1903–13 as a whole inventory investments were excessive. In any case, what may have been wasted here could not possibly have been prevented by feasible economic policy from the side of the British.

Gold and the monetary system

Table 2 records large investments in gold (species). Almost 20% of the capital available was invested in gold. Hoarding of gold may yield satisfaction to hoarders. Hoarding in this sense clearly took place. In Egypt, however, gold was mainly accumulated by the private sector, because since the monetary reform of 1885 Egypt was on a gold currency standard corresponding to a 100% gold reserve system. The establishment of a note-issuing bank, the

National Bank of Egypt (NBE) in 1898, with a 50% fractional reserve system (50% gold, 50% government securities) did not do much to change the system. Foreign trade (apart from some trade with ports in the Ottoman Empire) was based on modern means of payments, bills of exchange, trade bills, and so on, largely discounted abroad. Domestic transactions continued, however, to be based on (foreign) gold and silver coins. The notes of the NBE were accepted in unlimited amounts in payments to the government but were not made legal tender until the outbreak of World War I, when Egypt abruptly, and apparently without any difficulties, shifted from the gold currency standard to a (sterling) paper standard. When convertibility in gold was introduced in 1925 (the Egyptian pound following the pound sterling), there was no return to gold currency circulation, although nothing in principle stood in its way.

It goes without saying that the Egyptian monetary system before 1914 absorbed substantial amounts of capital that could have been used for other purposes. The actual value of gold coins in circulation in 1914 at the outbreak of the war is not known, but a figure of some LE 25–30 million in 1913 may be close to the mark.[22] With a pure paper standard this amount would, *ceteris paribus*, have been available for real investments. For the years 1903–13 it would suffice for industrial investments to almost four times the amount actually invested in industry. This, however, would obviously be wishful, anachronistic thinking. We are dealing with the era of the classical gold standard when a pure paper standard was not on the agenda. What we can historically think of is a fractional 50% gold reserve standard similar to the one established by the NBE in 1898 (copied upon the Bank of England system of 1844). Had the NBE been established already in 1885, the year of the Egyptian currency reform when the Egyptian pound was introduced as unit of account and its par value (gold content) was fixed, had the notes of the NBE been made legal tender from the very beginning and made compulsory means of payments at all transactions with the government, its enterprises, and agencies (taxes, fees, fares, public sector salaries, etc.), it is not inconceivable that the notes might have replaced gold currency in domestic transactions within a short time, say, before the turn of the century. The profits should not, of course, have been allowed to accrue to the NBE, but that could have been taken care of in the original concession, the *firman* establishing the company. Reforms such as these should not have been alien to the British, nor for that matter to the Egyptian government.[23] Successfully carried through, this reform would have freed sufficient re-

Table 4 · Industrial investments, 1903–13 and 1928–39
(cumulated, at 1903–13 prices, LE million)

	Machinery	Buildings	Total	Population (million)
Gross:				
1903–13	7.3	10.9	18.2	11.4
1928–39	11.8	22.8	34.7	15.5
Net:				
1903–13	1.0	5.7	6.7	11.4
1928–39	2.1	11.2	13.3	15.5

Source: Samir Radwan, "Capital Formation in Egyptian Industry and Agriculture, 1882–1967," Thesis, University of London, SOAS (September 1973), Tables 3.1, 3.2, 3.3. For 1928–39, my deflation.

sources for increasing industrial investment with some LE 10 to 15 million.

Industrialization, actual and potential

The low level of industrial investments until the 1930s is, of course, the main piece of evidence in favor of the lopsidedness criticism. By modern development standards, net industrial investments at the level 0.5%–1% of national income indicates a very low level of industrialization. Egypt's first five-year plan for 1959/60–1964/65 operated with an industrial gross investment–national gross value added ratio of about 7%. For 1903–13 the ratio may have been about 1.5%. It is, however, more relevant to compare with the period 1928–39, when industrialization was first inaugurated as a national policy behind the protection of the new tariff system.

Table 4 compares net and gross industrial investments for 1903–13 and 1928–39 with figures for total population. The data indicate a level of industrial investments in 1928–39 about double that in 1903–13, or, taking into account the population increase, about one and a half times the level in 1903–13. Company capital indicates a similar increase in industrial investments. Total capital (including reserves) in companies classified as industrial increased by LE 4.6 million during the years 1928–39 against 4.0 million during 1903–13.[24] For 1903–13, however, commerce and mining are included, and during the period 1928–39 larger amounts of bank credits may have been available for fixed investments than for 1903–13, thanks to the activities of Bank Misr.[25] I shall accept Radwan's figures at face value. As a basis for comparison I shall then assume that the industrialization that actually took place between 1928 and 1939 should have been accelerated and taken place already before World World I in addition to the actual industrialization at that time. Considering the increase in population, this would have required annual gross investments to run at a level LE 2.1 million higher and annual net investments LE 0.8 million higher than what actually happened before World War I. Since viable industries should be able to generate internal replacement financing, and incentives for replacement do exist if incentives exist for keeping the capital stock in place, the industrialization problem before World War I was to increase annual net investments from LE 0.8 to LE $0.8 + 0.8 = 1.6$ million.

The questions are now: Could and should domestic financing and incentives for such an increase in industrial investments have been created before World War I, considering the constraints of the Capitulations and looking at the problem from an Egyptian point of view? If these questions are answered in the affirmative, then we are on a solid ground for criticizing the British for not having promoted industrialization in Egypt.

The first question has already been answered in the affirmative in the previous section. Policies to put the country effectively on a fractional gold reserve standard, replacing gold currency circulation with note circulation, would supply more than sufficient capital for financing an additional investment program during the decade 1903–13 similar to that of the 1930s. Institutionally this might take the form of the establishment of an industrial bank (one of Tala'at Harb's early dreams), financed from the NBE on the basis of note circulation within the 50% gold cover rule. Both the NBE and the new industrial bank might need government guarantees, but otherwise it is hard to see why the monetary reform required should not be successful if pursued systematically and energetically by the government. Around 1900, Egypt was the only country in the world (excepting perhaps some less developed areas such as Yemen) remaining on a gold currency standard. As with anything perverse, Keynes was fascinated.[26] Notice that there is nothing inflationary in the proposal; it is simply a rationalization of the monetary system, replacing socially expensive gold coins with socially cheap paper notes at unchanged total money supply.

The second question is how to create incentives for the new

industrial investments to be made. With tariff reforms blocked by the Capitulations the only way to create incentives would have been through subsidizing industrial investments. In some ways that would actually be a better policy. Well-known welfare-theoretical arguments point to subsidies being superior to tariffs as a means of promoting industrialization. The problem is that subsidies from the government budget require revenues, and here again the capitulations were blocking the road. Fortunately, without violating the Capitulations, the monetary reform proposed here would not only provide the necessary domestic financing but would do so at zero interest rates. This opens up the possibility for the industrial bank, based on interest-free loans from the NBE, of advancing interest-free loans to industrial enterprises. I disregard administration costs which may have amounted to about one percent of the loans. The subsidy involved might correspond to, say, 7% per annum. At a capital-output ratio of, say, three, the interest subsidy would be equivalent to a production subsidy – or a tariff protection – of 21% measured on output. If we can judge from the experience during the 1930s, this should suffice to make production privately profitable for a number of important products. For 1936/37 nominal tariff rates were:[27]

Cotton yarns	9–17%
Cotton fabrics	23–28%
Cement	16%
Chemical products	8–20%
Paper products	3–13%
Leather products	15%
Shoes	36%

Despite the Great Depression, cotton textiles and chemical product companies paid impressive dividend rates in 1938:

Misr Spinning and Weaving	7%
Filature Nationale	11.54%
Ciment Portland de Helouan	10%
Ciment Portland-Tourah Cairo	10%
Salt and Soda	9.17%

while all industrial companies on average paid 7.17% dividends on their paid-up share capital.[28] The tariff reforms of 1930 and later were probably excessively protective.

Considering the basic 8% tariff rate permitted under the Capitulations, it would seem that these basic products, and industry more in general, profitable in the 1930s at the then existing tariff rates, would also have been profitable before World War I at 8% tariff rates if based on interest-free capital.[29]

Should industrialization have been accelerated before World War I?

Having now argued that a successful rationalization of the Egyptian monetary system might have sufficed for creating both domestic financing and incentives for additional industrialization before World War I without violating the Capitulations, the question is, of course, whether industrialization should have been accelerated at all. The additional domestic capital could perhaps have been invested better.

Contemporary nationalism in Egypt – Tala'at Harb is a good example – was apparently more concerned with liberating Egypt from the influence of foreign capital than with economic development *per se*. The capital set free through rationalization of the monetary system would, for instance, in 1913 have sufficed for open market purchases of a majority of ordinary shares in four leading banks in Egypt (Agricultural Bank, Credit Foncier, Land Bank, and NBE). Alternatively, the capital could have been used for repaying more than one tenth of the public debt if this had been thought to reduce foreign influence. In both cases the Egyptian national income would have increased (once) by 0.5% to 1% through the decline in interest and dividend payments to foreigners abroad. The returns would in both cases accrue to the central government budget and could be used for lowering taxes or increasing expenditure; only in the latter case would discrimination in favor of natives be possible.

One way of using the budgetary improvement entirely to the benefit of the native population would have been to create an elementary education system, designed for the broad population in urban and rural areas. It is generally acknowledged that elementary education was completely neglected by the British. Budgetary stringencies were part of the problem, and after the Anglo-French Agreement of 1904 appropriations for education did increase somewhat. It was not until after independence was initiated in 1923, however, that elementary education was made compulsory and serious efforts were made to establish a comprehensive system of education. It goes without saying that even today, after sixty years, the elementary education system is not really comprehensive. To build up a complete elementary education system takes gener-

ations. For that reason, if anything should have been accelerated it
was precisely education. It can even be argued, in particular in the
case of Egypt, that education was a necessary prerequisite for
successful industrialization.

One problem with industrialization in Egypt was, and still is, that
the country has few natural advantages for industry in the form of
industrial raw materials and (at that time, at least) energy; even the
famous Egyptian cotton did not provide Egypt with a natural advantage in cotton textiles. A comparison with India is in order
here.[30]

India, being a British colony (which Egypt never was) was politically even more tightly controlled than Egypt and was faced with
much the same free trade policies as Egypt. Yet, before the end of
the nineteenth century India had successfully developed three
basic, modern industries capable of competing in South and East
Asia with British industry. These industries were cotton spinning,
jute spinning and weaving, and iron and steel. The jute industry was
very much a British (Scottish) managed and financed venture.
Cotton textiles as well as iron and steel were, however, genuinely
native ventures (if "foreigners" were involved, it was mainly a
question of Parsees, for centuries settled in India and in a position
not without some resemblance to that of the "Levantines" in
Egypt). All three industries were based on local raw materials and
enjoyed substantial natural transportation advantages. The comparison between the Indian and Egyptian cotton textiles industries
is important here. The success of the Indian industry was limited
mainly to coarse yarns, an area in which the British were competed
out not only in the Indian but also in the Chinese market. Indian
cotton, of low quality and cheap, was ideal for the coarse yarns in
great demand from hand-weavers, supplying the poor masses in
India and China. Shipping Indian raw cotton to Lancashire and
returning coarse yarns gave Lancashire a strong disadvantage in
transportation costs, corresponding to some 25%–35% of the final
price. For fabrics and fine yarns, the Indian transportation advantage was (percentage-wise) much smaller, perhaps even nonexistent if the British products were based on American or Egyptian
cotton. Technologically, the Indians were superior, introducing
new American technology (the ring-frame and integrated production) decades before the British.

During its early years, from around 1860, the modern cotton
textiles industry in India enjoyed some modest tariff protection.
The protection was first lowered and then removed completely in

1882 (under pressures from Lancashire – Cromer was there), and when in 1895 a general 5% tariff was introduced (for revenue purposes), a countervailing excise tax was clamped on domestic cotton textiles, the model for the one imposed by Cromer in Egypt in 1901. The Indian cotton textiles industry did, however, enjoy some "protection" through the depreciation (by about 75%) of the silver rupee against sterling and other gold-standard currencies from about 1871 to 1894. How much the depreciation actually helped the Indian industry is disputed; Keynes argued, correctly, that it was at most a temporary protection.[31] In any case, this factor was eliminated when, from 1895, India was shifted on to the gold standard with some appreciation of the rupee. Thus from 1895 the Indian cotton textiles industry was without any form of artificial protection, yet it did very well (until the Japanese entered the stage).[32]

What the Indians successfully managed during the second half of the nineteenth century two foreign companies in Egypt failed to accomplish during the early years of the twentieth century, and when a partly indigenous Egyptian cotton textiles industry finally grew up in the 1930s, it was behind strongly protective barriers. As we have seen, the Indian modern cotton textiles industry did enjoy some protection during its formative period and thus may be considered a successful infant industry case. The early failure in Egypt of the cotton textiles industry was, however, due to a more basic problem than just lack of initial protection, a problem that continues to trouble Egyptian cotton textiles until this day. The very high quality (and price) of Egyptian cotton made it economical only as a raw material base for high-quality products (tire-duck, transmission belts, parachutes, fine clothing, etc.) for which there was little market in Egypt. If based on domestic cotton, the Egyptian cotton textiles industry would either have to produce low quality products based on expensive raw materials for the domestic market, or it would have to produce high-quality products for exports to Europe (which in effect meant the United Kingdom, one of the few countries where Egypt would not face tariff walls).

The early Egyptian cotton textiles industry made an attempt to produce coarse, cheap textiles for the domestic market, based on imported Indian raw cotton. With 8% tariffs on both imported raw cotton and imported Indian cotton textiles, Egypt clearly had a transportation disadvantage (quite apart from the infant industry problems, already overcome in India, not to mention Cromer's countervailing excise tax); the attempt was doomed to fail as, indeed, it did. In 1916, moreover, a ban on imported foreign cotton was introduced in Egypt (with the risk of importing foreign cotton diseases and insects as a pretext, but probably instigated by Egyptian cotton-growers). Production of high-quality goods for export would have required superior management, technical staff, and labor. It is here that the educational problem enters the picture. The managerial and technical problems were to some extent overcome when British multinationals (Bradford and Calico) joined forces with the Egyptian industry; but then, of course, Tala'at Harb was immediately accused of "selling out" to British capital. In any case, the common labor problem remained. The strong expansion in the 1930s of the cotton textiles industry, exclusively based on domestic cotton, was probably a serious mistake and there would have been no reason for making this mistake already before World War I. It might perhaps have made sense to subsidize the early cotton textiles industry, had it produced cheap coarse textiles for the domestic market on the basis of cheap imported cotton. (Anglo-Egyptian Spinning and Weaving did in fact borrow heavily from NBE in 1903. With interest-free loans it might have survived.) This industry would have needed much less protection than the industry actually established in the 1930s; the poor classes would have been supplied with textiles at much lower prices; the Egyptian cotton crop would have been fully exported and a surplus created over and above the payments for imported cotton. The possibility cannot be excluded, however, that Egypt should never have established a cotton textiles industry.

This, of course, raises the question of what the composition of an optimal industrialization program should have been. If in 1930 the government had chosen a protectionist program with a flat *ad valorem* rate of tariff or subsidy applied to all imports and exports (almost equivalent to a general currency depreciation), it could have been left to individual private agents to respond without the government setting priorities. With a discriminatory tariff system or an industrial bank giving interest free loans on a discretionary basis the government has to set priorities and select industries to be developed. Cotton textiles based on domestic cotton absorbed almost half the capital invested in industry from 1928 to 1939 simply because it was given sufficient protection. If that was a mistake, what else should have been developed? There were better alternatives. Cotton textiles based on imported cotton has been mentioned. Fine yarns for exports may have been a possibility: in the

1960s and 1970s yarns were successful in exports to the Soviet bloc. Cement could and should have been developed earlier and faster. Phosphate fertilizers later proved a successful industry and could have been developed much earlier. Pulp and paper are another example.[33] This much is clear: when protectionism finally came to Egypt in 1930, it was structured much more to please powerful, rent-seeking, special-interest groups than to serve the national interest. It is doubtful whether this could have been avoided with earlier industrialization based on interest-free loans from an industrial bank before World War I. This is just another reason why at that time the creation of a comprehensive elementary education system would have been preferable to industrialization, given both the capital and incentive constraints.

Conclusions

In terms of *Realpolitik* and considering the severe constraints for both raising domestic capital and creating incentives imposed by the Capitulations, it is far from obvious that accelerated industrialization should have been a high priority policy before World War I. Given the institutional and political framework it is not obvious that the British should be blamed for not promoting industrialization before 1914. It may even have been a blessing for Egypt that Cromer did his best to prevent the early development of a cotton textiles industry. What the British should be blamed for is *partly* letting an antiquated, expensive monetary system survive without serious attempts to reform, and *partly* ignoring the need for establishing a comprehensive educational system for the broad population. Both monetary and educational reform could and should have been undertaken. It is true that educational reform is very slow to yield returns in terms of income per capita. Fortunately, albeit by default rather than by design, the British hydraulic investments, biased in favor of labor and against land, made it possible for agriculture to absorb a substantial part of the population increase before World War II without a decline in real wages. Had a comprehensive educational system been established before World War I, the educational level of the population might at the end of the 1930s have been much more adequate for industrialization and made such policies more successful.

NOTES

1 Charles Issawi, "Egypt since 1800: A Study in Lopsided Development," *Journal of Economic History*, 21 (1961), 1–25.
2 Ibid.
3 T. B. Birnberg and S. A. Resnick, *Colonial Development: An Econometric Study* (New Haven and London: Yale University Press, 1975).
4 Bent Hansen, "Savings and Investments, Flow of Funds, Egypt, 1884–1913," Working Paper no. 135, Department of Economics, University of California, Berkeley (October 1979).
5 The export price index (Fisher, chained annually) declined by 36% from 1885 to 1898, but exceeded in 1913 the 1885 level by 49%. The corresponding import price index declined by 20% from 1885 to 1895, but in 1913 was 13% higher than in 1885. See Bent Hansen and E. F. Lucas, "Egyptian Foreign Trade, 1885–1961: A New Set of Trade Indices," *Journal of European Economic History*, 7 (1978), pp. 429–60.
6 Domestic savings include here savings made by members of the resident foreign community. The problem of how to account for resident foreigners in Egypt at that time is tricky and controversial. Standard national accounting considers all permanent residents as belonging to the country of residence. Foreign armed forces and administrations (diplomacy) are not considered permanent residents, however. The problem is thus confined to foreign civilians, residing permanently. So-called guest workers have made this a quantitatively big issue in Europe since World War II. In colonial times the issue was related mainly to foreign civilians residing permanently in a colony, enjoying special (extraterritorial) rights under the umbrella of the colonial power. Citizens of the Capitulary Powers under the jurisdiction of the Mixed Courts in Egypt are a case in point. Available information unfortunately does not permit us to single out this group statistically. The data leave no choice but to operate with this group as part of the domestic economy. Recent research on the industrialization process in Egypt during the interwar period (Robert L. Tignor, *State, Private Enterprise, and Economic Change in Egypt, 1918–1951* [Princeton, N. J.: Princeton University Press, 1984]) has led to a radical reevaluation, which I am inclined to support, of the role played by the foreign community in Egypt, a reevaluation that makes it natural in this case to follow standard national accounting recommendations. Be that as it may, it would have been preferable from many points of view to separate out this group statistically.
7 Bent Hansen, "Factor Prices in Egypt during the First Half of the Twentieth Century – with some International Comparisons," Working Paper no. 192, Department of Economics, University of California, Berkeley (February 1985), Appendix II.

8 Ibid., pp. 17–22; see below.

9 Property taxes in Cairo were increased from one-twelfth to one-tenth with an extension of the perimeter of the taxed area by Khedival decree in 1910, but only after approval by the Powers. Without approval of the Powers, modifications that would lower total revenue below LE 4 million could not be undertaken (decr. 18 Nov. 1904, Art. 36).

10 Jasper Yeates Brinton, *The Mixed Courts of Egypt* (rev. ed.; New Haven & London: Yale University Press, 1968), p. 178.

11 Issawi, "Egypt since 1800"; Tignor, *Economic Change in Egypt.*

12 E. R. J. Owen, *Cotton and the Egyptian Economy: A Study in Trade and Development* (Oxford: Clarendon Press, 1969), pp. 215–18.

13 W. Willcocks, *Egyptian Irrigation* (2nd ed.; London & New York: E. & F. Spon, 1899), pp. 173–5.

14 Major R. Hambury Brown, Introduction to Willcocks, *Egyptian Irrigation.*

15 Birnberg and Resnick, *Colonial Development.*

16 Gerry Dugay and Bent Hansen, "The Demand for American Cotton: An Econometric Disequilibrium Analysis with an Application to Egyptian Cotton," Working Paper no. 6, Institute of International Studies, University of California, Berkeley (April 1977).

17 Ahmed Abdel Wahab, *Memorandum on the Basis of a Stable Cotton Policy*, Memorandum submitted to H. E. the Minister of Finance (Cairo: Government Press, 1930).

18 For details see Hansen, "Factor Prices in Egypt," pp. 17–23.

19 Bent Hansen, "Interest Rates and Foreign Capital in Egypt under British Occupation," *Journal of Economic History*, 43 (December 1983), 867–84.

20 E. R. J. Owen, "The Cairo Building Industry and the Building Boom of 1897 to 1907," *Colloque International sur l'Histoire du Caire* (Cairo, 1969), pp. 337–50.

21 *The Egyptian Gazette*, June 8, 1907, p. 3.

22 Hansen, "Savings and Investments," pp. 7–9.

23 Bank of England should have a positive interest in monetary reform in Egypt: in 1906 outflow of gold to Egypt forced it to increase its rate of discount.

24 For 1928–39, *Statistique des sociétés anonymes, 1928 and 1939*; for 1903–12, A. E. Crouchley, *The Investment of Foreign Capital in Egyptian Companies and Public Debt*, Technical Paper no. 13, Ministry of Finance (Cairo: Government Press, 1936).

25 Eric Davis, *Challenging Colonialism, Bank Misr and Egyptian Industrialization, 1920–1941* (Princeton: Princeton University Press, 1983), ch. 6; Tignor, *Economic Change in Egypt*, chs. 4 and 5.

26 J. M. Keynes, *Indian Currency and Finance* (London: Macmillan & Co., 1913), pp. 1–3.

27 Robert Mabro and Samir Radwan, *The Industrialization of Egypt,*

1939–1973, Policy and Performance (Oxford: Clarendon Press, 1976), Table 4.1.

28 *Statistique des sociétés anonymes*, July 1939.

29 Fuel, the most important input, suffered a tariff rate of 4%. The effective rate of tariff may for most products have been on the order of 6% to 7%. Cromer's countervailing excise tax of 8% on domestically produced cotton textiles and some other products had no basis, of course, in the Capitulations.

30 The following paragraph is based mainly on Morris D. Morris, "The Growth of a Large-Scale Industry to 1947," in *The Cambridge Economic History of India*, Vol. II, c. *1957–c. 1970*, D. Kumar and M. Desai, eds. (Cambridge: Cambridge University Press, 1983), ch. 7.

31 Keynes, pp. 1–3.

32 Egyptian industrialization never enjoyed exchange depreciation protection. The country was put firmly on the gold standard in 1885. Had it remained on the old bimetallic standard, gold would probably have been replaced by silver in domestic transactions (Gresham's Law) and Egypt would have gone through a period of depreciation. To what extent that would have promoted industrialization in the 1880s and 1890s is difficult to say.

It is worth mentioning that Egypt, following the pound sterling, in 1925 took part in Churchill's disastrous revaluation of sterling. How much harm that did to Egyptian industrialization in the 1930s is also difficult to say; it certainly did harm to Britain. Probably the consequences were less severe in Egypt than in the United Kingdom because wages in Egypt were downwards flexible. Be that as it may, Tignor's statement (*Economic Change in Egypt*, p. 197), that "the linking of British and Egyptian currencies had served the Egyptian economy well up until 1939" is disputable.

33 I shall not go further into this topic here but only refer to an earlier study, Bent Hansen and Karim Nashashibi, *Foreign Trade Regimes and Economic Development, Egypt* (New York: National Bureau of Economic Research, 1975), chs. 8–10.

5 · On loyalties and social change

SAMIR KHALAF
Princeton University

History, to borrow Fernand Braudel's expressive metaphor, is like a river. On the surface it flows rapidly and disappears. But down below there is a deep stream which moves more slowly, does not change quickly, but is the more important because it drives the whole river. Braudel prods us to study, as he himself has admirably done, such deep currents particularly in elucidating processes of continuity and change in the evolution of societies.[1]

The focus of this paper, the pattern of loyalties and their impact on social change, allows one to probe into the nature and consequences of such deep undercurrents. Loyalties, particularly as they are manifested in sentiments, allegiances, and affiliations, are after all the basic ties which motivate, hold, and cement groups together within society. Accordingly, much of what happens in society may be understood by elucidating the character of loyalties and by identifying their impact on specific instances of social change. Fundamental as this matter is, there is still considerable ambivalence and uncertainty regarding the nature and pattern of these loyalties. As a result, we often misunderstand their character and misread some of their implications. Such misreading is not as benign and innocuous as often assumed. It should not be dismissed lightly as the inconsequential outcome of abstract scholars weaving conceptual images and paradigms in their intellectual sanctuaries and proverbial ivory towers. In some specific instances misreading has generated a large measure of distortion of sociohistorical realities. It has also led to some costly misadventures in schemes for socioeconomic planning and strategies for political development.

To this day, planners in the Arab world, as elsewhere in developing countries, continue to receive inconsistent advice. At times, in the name of secularization and rational planning, they are asked to erode, bypass, contain, or even devalue their traditional

89

loyalties. At other times, particularly when planners become mindful of the burgeoning tourist industry and commercial value of some of the rustic and colorful features of their folklore and popular culture, they are implored to preserve their threatened natural and cultural heritage. The very institutions and loyalties that were formerly devalued become coveted and prized attributes. Little wonder that traditional loyalties are either denigrated or idealized but rarely treated for what they actually are.

In certain instances political regimes are known to oscillate, often discordantly, between the two extremes. The initial exuberance they display for radical and total change, reinforced by an impetuous desire to efface the old order, quite often gives way to fatuous idealization of the past. The resurgence of Muslim fundamentalism and other reformist movements is, to a large extent, a reaction to excessive modernization. Such reactive movements, from quietist mystical orders to militant organizations, become more pronounced when modernization is associated with the "impurities" of Western incursions.

Clearly, scholars are not exempt from such charges and pitfalls. This is particularly apparent in the continuing discourse regarding the nature and direction of social change. After the initial upsurge in comparative studies of modernization, the field witnessed a decline during the mid and late seventies. The past few years, however, have seen a resurgence of interest and a revival of some of the earlier polemics.[2] Scholars are, once again, invoking the old issues as to whether there is any directionality in the process of modernization and to what extent it is possible to justify the idea of a singular path or end to that process.

Within the context of this paper, the issue becomes one of ascertaining the nature of the interplay between so-called "modern" and "traditional" loyalties. Are these loyalties as polarized and dichotomous as often suggested? Is it necessary for Arab societies, particularly those characterized by a large measure of persistence in their traditional values and institutions, to experience an erosion in these "survivals" before they can become receptive to societal and behavioural transformations?

The literature on comparative modernization and social change is still riddled with ambiguities and often inconsistent responses to basic questions of this sort. Except for a few noted and recent departures, the bulk of the literature, as I have suggested elsewhere, has remained essentially within the fold of the Western intellectual tradition of European and American sociology.[3] Assumptions regarding the directionality of change and the inevitable erosion of traditional loyalties by the irreversible forces of secularization, the polarization of tradition and modernity as incompatible dichotomies, or the denigration of traditions as useless and nostalgic survivals, are clearly not the global models they are often claimed to be. The pitfalls involved in transposing such allegedly universal models on other instances of social change are serious.

There is no need to repeat here the charges leveled against these perspectives, which were prevalent during the 1950s and 1960s. This has been convincingly and amply done by a score of other writers.[4] It is sufficient to note that they are patently inadequate in helping us understand the nature of the interplay between traditional and modern loyalties. Indeed, they actually distort certain sociohistorical realities so distinctive of particular Arab societies. For at no point in the recent history of the Arab world, even in so-called revolutionary and radical regimes, have the processes of change been so total and all-embracing that they swept aside all the vestiges of their traditional past. Nor have traditional values and institutions been so immobile and obstructive as to pose unsurmountable barriers to social change or to require that these values be rendered inoperative by encapsulating or neutralizing their "polluting" impact.

The moral to be extracted from these and other critical reassessments of the extensive literature on comparative modernization is plain and clear. We need to divest ourselves of the conceptual and ideological tyranny of these models. If we are to employ the indispensable Weberian ideal-typical contrast between "traditional" and "modern," then, in the words of Reinhard Bendix, we should "deideologize" these constructs in such a way as not to impart "a spurious, deductive simplicity to the transition from one to the other."[5]

We clearly need an alternative approach for the analysis of the interplay between tradition and modernity. For neither in their antecedents, nor in their patterns and consequences, do processes of change in the Arab world comply with the Western experience or with the options or courses taken by other newly developing nations. We need an approach, to repeat, which neither anticipates the ultimate purgation of traditional "survivals" nor regards traditional loyalties as incompatible with modernization. That is, we need an approach which recognizes the possibility, in certain contexts, of the continuing coexistence and mutual reinforcement of tradition and modernity, and which makes for greater opportunities for congruence and overlapping whereby tradition and modernity are allowed to infiltrate and transform each other. It is in this sense that the interplay between tradition and modernity is conceived more as a dialectical than a dichotomous relationship. The purpose of this essay is to provide further theoretical and empirical evidence in favor of this dialectical approach. First, the case for the dialectical character of tradition and modernity is elaborated. Second, an attempt is made to disclose the nature of adaptive modernization and the type of agencies or institutions most effective in bringing it about.

The case for dialectics: sustained change and social cohesion

The case for a dialectical approach requires little in the way of theoretical justification. There is no need, in fact, for elaborate models or complex reformulations of earlier conceptual schemes. Several basic but viable analytical tools already exist which may be appropriately employed in analyzing structural and institutional changes without the moral premises and ethnocentric biases inherent in some of the conventional perspectives. Concepts such as John Lewis's distinction between "adaptive" and "inverse" modernization, Clifford Geertz's "involution," Rustow and Ward's "reinforcing dualism," S. N. Eistenstadt's "patrimonialism," or Ernest Gellner's analysis of "post-traditional" forms in Islam, to mention a few, are all instances of the kind I have in mind.

John Lewis employs notions of structural differentiation and role proliferation in his analysis of the social limits to politically induced change. His distinction between adaptive and inverse modernization is particularly relevant. Adaptive modernization comprises "the gradual, unplanned and essentially spontaneous differentiation of roles and the gradual evolution of formal modes of organization."[6] In essence, this involves the gradual proliferation of roles and the progressive development from simple, undifferentiated, premodern institutions (predominantly defined according to particularistic and local standards) to more specialized, complex, and differentiated ones. Since many of the premodern social institutions and relationships are "carried over" – particularly those which help shape the attitudes of individuals – social cohesion is maintained during the unsettling period of social change.

Inverse modernization, on the other hand, occurs "where the gradual processes of change are bypassed and specialized organizational forms are directly transferred to new nations under the guidance of a revolutionary or modernizing elite." In some respects this involves the "inversion" of those processes of development which underlie adaptive modernization. The often impetuous revolutionary elites of new nations, according to Lewis, are not only bent on a disruptive and rapid course of modernization, but have consciously repudiated the premodern social relationships which might help sustain minimal social cohesion. In this way, "they exacerbate disorder and destroy potential support: they thereby sow the seeds of their own destruction. Left unchecked, these difficulties would produce extreme social upheaval and a new revolutionary situation."[7]

In analyzing processes of agricultural and ecological change in Indonesia, Clifford Geertz borrows the interesting concept of involution from the American anthropologist Alexander Goldenweister, who devised it to describe

those cultural patterns which, after having reached what would seem to be a definitive form, nonetheless fail either to stabilize or transform themselves into a new pattern but rather continue to develop by becoming internally more complicated [...] What we have here is pattern plus continued development. The pattern precludes the use of another unit or units, but it is not inimical to play within the unit or units. The inevitable result is progressive complication, a variety within uniformity, virtuosity within monotony. This is involution. A parallel instance [...] is provided by what is called ornateness in art, as in the late Gothic. The basic forms of art have reached finality, the structural features are fixed beyond variation, inventive originality is exhausted. Still development goes on. Being hemmed in on all sides by a crystallized pattern, it takes the function of elaborateness. Expansive creativeness having dried up at the source, a special kind of virtuosity takes its place [...].[8]

Involution in the case of Indonesia was highly functional because it enabled the society to "evade, adjust, absorb, and adapt but not really change." Since the particular Javanese village Geertz explored was shaped by forces over which it had little control and since it was denied the means for actively reconstructing itself, it

clung to the husks of selected established institutions and limbered them internally in such a way as to permit greater flexibility, a freer play of social relationships within a generally stereotyped framework [...] The quality of everyday existence in a fully involuted Javanese village is comparable to that in the other formless human community, the American suburb: a richness of social surfaces and a monotonous poverty of social substance.[9]

Certain institutions, roles, and other seemingly traditional patterns of behavior in the Arab world can be said to be "involuted" in a related if not completely identical sense. In Lebanon, for example, family firms, family associations, and communal and voluntary organizations have displayed considerable degrees of internal adaptability while retaining their outward fixity.[10] Similar tendencies are manifested in the persistence of patron–client networks,[11] Sufi orders, brotherhoods, urban quarters, and reformist movements.[12] In most of these instances the outer form, the social surface of these organizations has remained fundamentally the same, while their inner substance managed to undergo appreciable differentiation and development. The concept of involution is relevant and useful precisely because it recognizes the possibility of internal differentiation, variety, development, and a certain measure of "virtuosity," while cultural patterns retain their definitive and crystallized form. Outward fixity and inner dynamism, in other words, coexist and reinforce each other.

Rustow and Ward identify the quality of reinforcing dualism to explain Japan's classic and perhaps most dramatic instance of the systematic and purposeful exploitation of traditional institutions for the achievement of modernizing goals. They provide ample evidence to falsify the conventional thesis by showing that the role of traditional attitudes and institutions in the modernizing process has often been "more symbiotic than antagonistic." The most conspicuous example of this reinforcing dualism is the political role of the emperor:

> Here is an institution which is not only traditional but archaic. Yet when faced with the problem of constituting a modern nation-state in Japan, it was possible for the Meiji leadership to exhume this ancient institution, imbue it with quite a new content and much higher degree of visibility and status, and emerge with an extraordinarily effective symbol and instrument of national unity, discipline and sacrifice.[13]

Similar instances of reinforcing dualism are evident in the economic field. The maintenance of small traditionally organized units of production alongside the most modern factories seem to have contributed to the rapid and effective economic development of Japan. The obvious conclusion Rustow and Ward draw from this is clear: "many elements of the traditional society could be converted into supports for the process of political modernization. The result was added impetus of a sort conducive to modernization."[14]

Eisenstadt's concept of patrimonialism, particularly as it relates to the persistence of patron–client networks, feudal and semi-feudal survivals, and other personalistic loyalties and associations, can also be judiciously applied to explore concrete instances of the reinforcing character of the interplay between traditional and modern forms.[15] According to Eisenstadt, this perspective discloses the inadequacies of some of the basic premises of the earlier theories of modernization on at least four counts:

first, by showing that many of these societies and states did not develop in the direction of certain modern nation-states; second, by demonstrating that these regimes did not necessarily constitute a temporary "transitional" phase along an inevitable path to this type of modernity; third, by indicating that there was nevertheless some internal "logic" in their development, and last by emphasizing that part, at least, of this logic or pattern could be understood from some aspects of the traditions of these societies and derived from them.[16]

Two other relatively obscure but equally telling examples of the dialectics I have in mind may also be cited. To document the adaptation of traditional Islamic movements to modern conditions, Ernest Gellner provides an insightful analysis of two other paradoxical but successful instances of so-called post-traditional forms in Islam: the Ismailis of the Shiᶜa, and the Murids, a Sufi brotherhood in the Senegal.[17] The first group operates conceptually outside the bonds of Sunni orthodoxy, the second claims to have remained within it. Neither group, however, is particularly predisposed to the allegedly rational, universalistic, and achievement-oriented ethics of the modern world. Yet both have displayed remarkable entrepreneurial and organizational skills, while sustained by mystical beliefs and primordial loyalties which are the antithesis of the Weberian model of the Protestant Ethic. In each case, Gellner concludes:

A fortunate combination of circumstances has enabled a particular set of organizational and ideological elements, inherited from a tradition in which they were but slight variants of a standard pattern, to make a marked impact in novel circumstances. Shiᶜism is an unpromising candidate for the Protestant Ethic, but the followers of the Aga Khan are famed as entrepreneurs, and it seems unlikely that without their Shiᶜa faith, they could have been as successful as in fact they have been. Sufism does not resemble socialism and looks like most unpromising ideological equipment for the formation of agricultural kibbutzim, but, in its Murid form, this is just what is has achieved [...] In either case, an explanation in terms of the faith alone and its preaching is woefully inadequate, but in either case, the faith played a crucial part.[18]

Finally, several other instances of the dialectical relationship between tradition and modernity are increasingly recognized lately.

At least two recent expressions can be noted here. One has to do with the role of informal groups, kinship networks, and other primordial ties in political development. James Bill and Carl Leiden provide persuasive evidence of the pervasiveness and profound influence these networks continue to have on political loyalties, power struggle, in relaying vital political information, and in arriving at consequential political decisions.[19] The other focuses on the developmental potential of indigenous and other traditional grassroots organizations in the formation of viable cooperatives, collectivities, and other peasant associations concerned with various rural development projects ranging from rotating credit and saving associations to the construction, maintenance, allocation, and management of water schemes and irrigation projects.

For Nash, Dandler, and Hopkins, cooperatives are conceived as communities which demonstrate how people direct themselves to form, out of the old human material, new institutions to cope with their changing world. They, too, speak of the "dialectic between structure and movement" and how "new forms of mobilization relate to existing traditional structures." They provide supportive evidence, from various cross-cultural settings, to demonstrate "the effectiveness of this kind of grafting of new organizations on the traditional kinship and communal organizations."[20]

Likewise Cernea, Siebel and Massing, and Colletta, among others, provide further substantive evidence along those lines. Cernea is quite explicit and maintains that policymakers or development practitioners in this area tend to develop one of two basic sets of attitudes:

> The first consists of ignoring or underestimating the development function or potential of grass roots, production-oriented peasant organizations. This is the well-known attitude of certain national development agencies that perceive indigenous organizations and culture as a constraint on modernization, as a remnant of old times, and a nuisance to be eliminated, in order to really "modernize."
> The second consists of idealizing the traditional organizations and culture and ignoring the historical necessity of changing them too; this is tantamount to not understanding the essence of organizational forms as a cultural adaptive mechanism to change and as a sociocultural form for absorbing and utilizing modernized technologies.[21]

For Cernea, clearly, neither of these two positions can guide, either in practical or in theoretical terms, an effective development policy. Instead of regarding traditional organizations as a constraint, could they not, Cernea asks, be utilized as a resource for development? "A sound modernization policy should make the best use of all available resources [. . .] when they are amenable to development activities. On the other hand, the need to strengthen, change, and develop these organizations themselves should not be overlooked."[22]

Colletta makes a similar plea for the use of indigenous culture. He concludes his Indonesian case study by writing:

All too often development has confronted culture as a bulwark of conservatism, infrequently looking towards its potential use for positive change. Anthropologists have been quick to document the confrontation between development and culture [. . .] [instead of] leading the creative discovery of how long-established cultural pathways of interaction, established roles, institutions and value incentive systems might be employed as levers for positive change.[23]

This charge does not apply to at least one anthropologist, Elizabeth Fernea, who after an absence of five years revisited the Arab world and returned to speak of "new voices." In her recent book, an edited volume of evocative essays, stories, poems, life histories, and so on, she argues that despite the rich variety of expressions, there is a great shift in the aspirations of men and women:

No longer is the example of the West seen as the answer to the problems of the Middle East [. . .] People are attempting to improve their lives through indigenous traditions and customs; through the dominant religion of the area, Islam; and through their own kinship and family patterns. They are improvising and combining the new and the old, adapting, changing, and building, trying to create their own form of independence.[24]

In the Arab world, these new voices are far from new: they have always been there. Somehow, social scientists and historians failed to identify or recognize their true nature or the role they could play in generating and absorbing change. In fact, a generation of earlier scholars had either denigrated the presence of such traditional values and sentiments or prodded Arabs to disengage themselves from them, if they were to enjoy the fruits of modernity.[25]

Further instances of the mutual reinforcement of tradition and modernity, from both developed and developing societies, can be easily furnished.[26] The foregoing examples are, it is hoped, sufficient to establish the fact that such a dialectic is much more widespread and viable than has so far been admitted by interested observers. The oversight is understandable and may be accounted for in two ways. First, as has been suggested earlier, because of the predominance of certain Western perspectives and the emergence of radical revolutionary elites in the Third World, we have either overlooked or denigrated the modernizing potential of traditional loyalties and institutions. Simply not enough social scientists have been trained to look for, recognize, and document this convergence. Second, forging a blend between seemingly discordant elements is admittedly difficult. At least it has not always been a simple and manageable task. These historical forces – the desire for continuity and change, for coherence and dynamism, for institutional transformation and cultural reconstruction, for "essentialism" and "epochalism,"[27] to mention a few of the many labels applied to this interplay – are impelled after all by different sentiments and values and often derive their support from divergent and disparate social groups.

The experience of specific countries may vary, but the tensions and the broad patterns bespeak of essentially the same process or underlying concern: how to preserve cherished values and loyalties while transforming the institutional and material basis of society. Expressed more pointedly: how is social cohesion to be maintained if change is accelerated?

Rather than looking in either of two directions – the rooted traditions of the past, or the more secular and liberal components – several countries in the Arab world have been inclined toward grafting or reconciling the two dimensions. The results may often seem as an incoherent and precarious mélange of disparate elements. They have been, however, particularly at the micro and local level, effective in generating and sustaining change while maintaining social cohesion and some measure of cultural continuity.

Features of adaptive modernization

Three central features of adaptive modernization may be extracted from the discussion thus far. All three are essential for understanding and justifying the need for a dialectical perspective.

1. No matter how modernization is defined, it most certainly involves the will and capacity of a society to absorb and generate change or innovation. The capability for sustained growth, however, need not involve total and radical transformation. Nor should it necessitate incessant adoption and borrowing of new ideas and practices. Innovation can take place through the restructuring and

rearrangement of existing institutions. Indeed, the distinctive feature of adaptive modernization is the capacity of existing institutions and agencies to rearrange themselves to confront new challenges and cope with continuing tensions and problems. In brief, a large measure of modernization can and does take place by mobilizing traditional networks and loyalties.

2. Another distinctive attribute of modernization stands out. Whether the process assumes a gradualist and spontaneous course or a more radical and revolutionary reconstruction, whether it originates from internal indigenous forces or from external social contact, modernization always generates discontinuities, imbalances, and tensions which necessitate adjustments and continuous adaptation. No mode of social interaction is free from the occasional ramifications of internal tension. Accordingly, another feature of modernity is the capacity of a society to cope with the discontinuities and discrepancies inherent in a changing social order.[28]

3. Modernity, as Rousseau poignantly realized more than 200 years ago, despite all its potential promises, remains a disruptive social process and a bitter and agonizing personal experience. If one is to be mindful of some of its disquieting by-products – alienation, apathy, homelessness, overurbanization, excessive materialism, pollution, senseless rebellion, pointless crime and deviance, and so on – there must be more cognizance of the need for stabilizing and integrative mechanisms which could provide some measure of social support and psychic reinforcement. The will to be modern, after all, and the desire to enjoy the material benefits of modernity are not the only overpowering urges among newly developing societies. Equally compelling is the will to survive with dignity and honor, or what Mazzini called the "need to exist and have a name." In fact, the concern for national consciousness, cultural identity, and personal autonomy appears to be assuming more prominence than the heedless craving for unlimited growth and material progress.

If we accept these fundamental components, then modernization becomes ultimately a question of which are the appropriate agencies capable of generating change and absorbing and mediating tensions without threatening national identity. The viability and effectiveness of any agency of modernization should be assessed in terms of its propensity for providing these basic elements. In this sense, modernization, contrary to what is often assumed,[29] requires more than the expansion of production and communication, the broadening of loyalties from family, village, and community to nation, the secularization of public life, the rationalization of political authority, the promotion of functionally specific organizations, and the substitution of achievement criteria for ascriptive ones. These are no doubt essential for absorbing and generating change, but it is doubtful whether they are similarly effective in coping with imbalances while retaining a sense of national identity and social integration. Of equal importance is the capacity of a system to incorporate traditional social groupings which could act as palliatives in absorbing some of the imbalances and in maintaining some measure of political consciousness and national identity. In concluding his lucid and exhaustive survey of the economic history of the Middle East, Charles Issawi singles out this contradiction as a future source of social and political unrest in the region.[30] Peoples of the Middle East, he maintains, much like those of the rest of the world, are seeking to achieve incompatible aims: economic growth, higher levels of living, national power and equality, a greater sense of community, cultural identity, and political liberty.

Modernization, then, should not be taken to mean necessarily the erosion of traditional loyalties and groupings, or a process of "disengagement from traditions."[31] It is doubtful whether specific countries in the Arab world, or elsewhere for that matter, could ever sustain substantial change and development if these transformations were to dislodge the rooted traditional interests and loyalties. Likewise, modernization need not involve the emergence of exclusively rational and secular agencies. Ultimately it means that all groups – traditional and rational, secular and confessional, communal and national – become increasingly group-conscious and aware of their particular interests.

It is primarily because of such consideration that the central thesis of this essay argues in favor of an adaptive and reconciliatory form of modernization. At the risk of oversimplification, one may argue that the basic problem of modernization, in many parts of the Arab world, has been and will continue to be one of convergence and assimilation: how to assimilate some of the rational instruments of a nation-state into the fabric of social orders which are still sustained by primordial allegiances and particularistic loyalties. The former are necessary for development, the latter for social and psychic reinforcement. Both, however, are necessary for sustaining modernization.

What is being suggested here is that insofar as modernization, to some extent, is a disruptive process, the effectiveness of a modernizing agency should not be measured solely in terms of its capacity to absorb and generate change. Of equal importance, as was suggested earlier, is its capacity to cope with tensions and discontinuities and to promote a certain measure of cultural identity and national consciousness.

This is not a trivial matter. Much of the tension Arab societies face today can be attributed to their failure in meeting the basic dimensions outlined above. The specific experience of particular societies could, in fact, be differentiated in terms of their predisposition in satisfying such attributes.

The particular roles and institutional arrangements which the Lebanese have devised at various stages of their history, for example, kinship associations, various forms of political patronage, parochial voluntary organizations, family firms, and the like are a case in point.[32] While these mediating structures have been effective in generating change and alleviating some of the tensions and disquieting effects of modernization, they have not been successful in generating the necessary conditions that sustain civic ties and national loyalties. The very factors which account for much of the vitality, resourcefulness, and integration of the Lebanese are also the factors responsible for the erosion of civic ties and national loyalties.

Expressed differently, loyalties that enable in some respects, disable in other respects. This notion or distinction can be appropriately applied both to account for the failure of specific instances of socioeconomic planning and development, and to underscore the deeper and more encompassing predicament other countries in the Arab world are also facing. It also clarifies the inherently ambivalent and inconsistent character of the interplay between traditional and modern loyalties. In some instances, traditional loyalties have acted as leavens in reinforcing and supporting national planning, economic resourcefulness, and industrial development. In others, they have often obstructed the process of social change and retarded the growth of national or higher forms of social consciousness. This double supportive-subversive function is readily apparent; a few illustrations will suffice.

The relatively low incidence of social disorganization and deviant behavior, particularly as reflected in rates of crime and delinquency, drug addiction, alcoholism, suicide, and other symptoms of alienation and anomie, may to a large extent be attributed to the survival of primordial, kinship, and communal ties in the Arab world. As repeated studies have shown, the social and psychological supports people continue to derive from such ties have insulated rapidly urbanizing districts from the temporal, segmented, and impersonal types of social contacts often associated with urbanism.[33] Likewise, patron–client networks, in a variety of sociopolitical settings, continue to offer access to vital services, personal benefits, and privileges.[34] The same is true of the role of parochial voluntary associations, urban quarters, and religious orders. But it is the survival of loyalties and mediating structures that also accounts for much of the deficiency in civility and in higher and more encompassing forms of national consciousness from which Arab societies continue to suffer. In short, the factors that enable at the micro and communal level, disable at the macro and national level.

In virtually all parts of the Arab world the pattern and direction of social change will ultimately depend on how or when this dilemma will be resolved. Indeed in some societies, in Lebanon in particular, the country's political future has become inextricably linked with such a predicament. At the risk of overgeneralization, I am suggesting that sociopolitical systems which continue to display strong tribal, ethnic, or sectarian pluralism and where subnational loyalties often supersede national commitments have much in common. They all need those sociopolitical institutions or structural arrangements which will permit the average Lebanese to preserve some of his primordial allegiances without threatening the already precarious and tenuous national sentiments and loyalties. This, among other things, will necessitate the development of a new political and national leadership, one that will encourage and sanction extensive political resocialization and restructuring of certain existing values and loyalties. Without restructuring or resocialization, these political entities cannot possibly develop into a full-fledged nation-state. Compared to the purely secular or traditional institutions, the adaptive agencies I have in mind could still potentially be more effective in being the carriers of these transformations, particularly if reinforced by resocialization.

That these adaptative agencies or mediating structures have survived for so long is one indication that they continue to answer some durable and profound needs. That some of them degenerate or cannot as effectively mobilize and integrate human and other resources at higher levels of the social order is, in many respects, inevitable and predictable, given the pluralistic and multifarious nature of group affiliations in the Arab world. Such realities, as Durkheim often reminds us, are reasons to seek the reformation of these agencies, not to declare them forever useless, or to destroy them.[35]

Alternative courses of modernization

If the postulated features of modernization are accepted as central to the understanding of the interplay between loyalties and social change, then the focus of analysis should be directed towards those mediating structures which display the highest propensity for innovation, for coping with some of the imbalances and disruptive consequences of change, and finally for integrating the social order and retaining a measure of group identity and solidarity. This is emphasized because there is a tendency in the literature to overrate the innovative aspects of modernization at the expense of the integrative and tension-reducing capacity of a particular agency or system. Once again, I reiterate that because of the persistence of certain perspectives on social change with their associated emphasis on rationality, growth, and development, some of the integrative and sociocultural dimensions of modernization are often overlooked or treated only obliquely. Accordingly, the central problem of how social cohesion is to be maintained if change is accelerated continues to be generally ignored.[36]

If this is the context – that is, sustained change and social cohesion – within which modernization is to be evaluated, then one of three alternative courses of modernization becomes possible:

1. Specific Arab countries could, as some have already done, adopt a coercive and disciplined model in line with many newly emerging nations where the state becomes the dominant agency of political socialization and modernization. In a Marxian sense, the state will presumably liberate man from his communal and primordial ties and establish collective allegiance on the basis of the "unmediated loyalties" and devotions of individuals.[37] All voluntary associations, special-purpose groups, and social identities – traditional and rational alike – will be eroded or become virtually nonexistent. This unmediated approach to modernization (for lack of a better expression it can be so labeled) has not only been badly battered by academic critics, it has been faulted by events. Suffice it to note here that given the pluralistic and persisting tribal structure of Arab societies, let alone the resurgence of fundamentalism in its various forms, this option cannot possibly gain any widespread appeal. The totalitarian or authoritarian model is certainly effective

in generating social cohesion and solidarity, but only at the expense of sealing off all avenues of individuality and self-expression. Increasing centralization and state control may produce the desired goals of political stability and uniformity, but only by insulating the individual from modern life. Among other things, citizens in such a system are incapable of imagining any other values except those defined by the state. Also, this model assumes that becoming modern is inherently revolutionary, in that it seeks to dislodge all the inherited basic institutions, a process that can only be carried out by, and under the guidance of, a radical elite.[38]

Durkheim, once again, can be appropriately invoked here. "When the state," he warns us, "is the only environment in which men can live communal lives, they inevitably lose contact, become detached, and thus society disintegrates. A nation can be maintained only if, between the state and the individual, there is intercalated a whole series of secondary groups near enough to the individuals to attract them strongly in their sphere of action and drag them, in this way, into the torrent of social life."[39]

The critical question, then, is what sort of groups are more effective in "dragging," to use Durkheim's expression, individuals into the torrent of social life. Within this context, any authoritarian or centralized model that requires the elimination of such mediating groups is clearly the most perilous course a country can take.

2. Countries could opt for a more liberal and secular approach where change is mediated through predominantly rational agencies of modernization, and where political allegiance and loyalty are sustained by the civic instruments of a nation state. The majority of Western scholars, particularly in their earlier writings, were inclined to favor this approach. Daniel Lerner, Edward Shils, Manfred Halpern, Karl Deutsch, S. N. Eisenstadt, to mention a few, all identify the agencies of political development in terms of the instruments of the nation-state modeled after the experience of some Western countries.[40] Modern man, whether through "empathy," "psychic mobility," or socioeconomic "mobilization" is defined in terms of psychological attitudes which predispose him toward secular, pragmatic, instrumental, and utilitarian ties and contacts. He is also a "participant" man in that he experiences modern citizenship by joining political associations or special-purpose groups. Accordingly, there is extensive consideration of the role of the mass media, the military elite, political parties, civil bureaucracy, and other so-called institutional vectors of modernization,[41] but hardly any recognition of the role of adaptive agencies

in bringing about political development or promoting cultural identity and social integration. Secular institutions are seen as liberating agencies that free or disengage man from traditional loyalties and prepare him psychologically for modernity. Both of these notions – the one of instrumentality and utilitarianism and the other of participation in secular political groups – do not correspond to realities or characteristics of social change in most Arab societies. Even if they were to exist, the rational instruments of change are of doubtful value in coping with the imbalances and discontinuities inherent in a changing society. Neither can they be effective, as suggested earlier, as integrative mechanisms.

The early experience of some of the revolutionary and radical regimes in the Arab world is instructive in this regard. Their leaders were more than eager to adopt purely secular schemes in launching programs and projects for restructuring the socioeconomic, cultural, and administrative resources in their countries. Many of these projects, intended as models and showpieces of collective will and rational planning, in fact became sources of public embarrassment and failure shortly after their implementation. The Tahrir Province, during the earlier period of the Nasserite regime in Egypt, is one such dramatic and costly instance.

Launched in 1954 as an experiment in desert reclamation and land reform, the Tahrir project was intended to cast the state in the role of social engineer to create new group relations and new roles which the rest of the society could emulate.[42] The architects of the project were so exuberant and excessive in their blueprints, so utopian in their conceptions, that they overlooked some of the most common everyday life realities and basic loyalties which have characterized the life of the Egyptian peasant for so long. In a utopian, almost "Brave New World" fashion, peasants were made to live in rows of detached residential units on grid-net streets named after war heroes. They woke to military music and were expected to dispense their labor collectively with elected cooperatives to process and market their produce. These and other equally bizarre features prompted Nasser himself, in 1965, to publicly criticize the project as an example of muddled planning and confused thinking.[43]

This is not an isolated occurrence; other examples of excessive rationalization and corresponding insensitivity to indigenous needs and local traditions abound. For example, misguided attempts at mobilizing and structuring the labor force and creating national unions and Pan-Arab labor federations,[44] family planning programs and population policy,[45] and social welfare agencies and benevolent associations have been frequently ruinous and devastating in their impact. The most striking attempt, perhaps, is in the area of urban and town planning, where the imposition of colonial principles of spatial order and subsequent urban strategies have often led to conflicting and inconsistent planning schemes. This is particularly true in North Africa, where efforts to preserve and devalue "native" institutions inevitably created dualistic and jarring juxtapositions of striking different urban structures.[46]

3. The third and perhaps most realistic and effective alternative is the particularistic or adapative path to modernity. This approach does not exclude the possibility of mobilizing traditional groupings in the process of modernization. It is an adaptive course in more than one sense. First, because it attempts to mediate change through agencies which are not exclusively rational or secular. Second, it employs efforts to reconcile some of the universal and rational principles to the indigenous cultural traditions.

It is primarily for these reasons that the predisposition to justify change within traditional contexts should not be dismissed as a conservative gesture to glorify the sacred traditions of the past. Recognizing the viability of some primordial ties and loyalties should not be taken to mean that one seeks refuge in his past heritage and communal attachments to escape confrontation with the contemporary challenges of the modern age. The adaptive path to modernity is not a resigned and nostalgic flight. Rather, it emanates from a given sociohistorical reality, a reality that cannot be ignored or simply willed away by prophetic visions of a secular social order free of all primordial attachments. Putting new wine in old bottles, to borrow a trite metaphor, can be quite salutary in absorbing conflict and in facilitating the acceptance of new ideas. Furthermore, the fact that an agency is traditional in form or structure does not imply that it must espouse traditional values, or that it must devote itself exclusively to passing on sacred values or preserving traditional lore and skills. Conversely, a seemingly modern institution, or exposure to modern values and practices, is no guarantee that man will undergo a drastic transformation in his spirit and that he will, after all, acquire modern life-styles.

The case for adaptive modernization can be justified on at least one additional ground. There is a tendency in the literature to exaggerate the differences and discontinuities between so-called modern and traditional loyalties. For example, Karl Deutsch sees the transition from one polarity to the other as a "process in which major clusters of old social, economic, and psychological commitments are eroded and broken and people become available for new patterns of socialization and behavior."[47] Inkeles asserts that one of the marks of the contemporary man is that "he will no longer live enmeshed in a network of primary kin ties [. . .] but rather will be drawn into a much more impersonal and bureaucratic milieu."[48]

The basic argument of this essay departs from the tradition of dichotomous schemes, a tempting and powerful tradition, which still occupies a peculiar place in the folklore of Western sociological theory. Indeed, we cannot begin to understand what is involved in the processes of social change in the Arab world unless we abandon the tendency to view transformation as an inevitable, directional, and unilinear movement from one polar end of the scheme to the other. Despite their rich insights, all such polarized dichotomies obscure and mystify the inherently dialectical character of the relationship between traditional and rational loyalties.

To repeat, then, we cannot think of modernization in terms of a qualitative decline in traditional loyalties and the emergence of modern ones. We must consider instead what mixture, or rather what blend of traditional and modern patterns is most effective in meeting the three dimensions of modernization outlined earlier. In a sense, we can think of modern patterns as providing the superstructure, and thus conclude that effective modernization depends upon whether the traditional patterns reinforce or undermine the superstructure of modernity. This is certainly a far more value-neutral approach than the ones which ipso facto declare the obstructive and unchanging character of all traditional values and institutions.

Both historical and more recent evidence appears to suggest that change mediated through exclusively traditional or exclusively rational agencies is not likely to be continuous or effective. Indeed, most such efforts have only generated inauspicious and extremist reactions: either the mindless denigration of traditional loyalties, or their fatuous idealization. For Ernest Gellner, the ideological consequences of this predicament are obvious. These societies are usually torn between two trends or temptations, Westernization and populism, that is, the idealization of the local folk tradition. "The old local 'Great Tradition' is generally damned by its failure to resist the West and by its doctrinal and organizational rigidity, once a source of strength, now a great weakness."[49]

Quite often, in fact, the two trends are coterminous. The excessive or premature introduction of rational or secular norms and lifestyles, Western-inspired or otherwise, begets or exacerbates revivalist and fundamentalist reactions. The chasm and tension between these two extremes have been responsible recently for some of the most disruptive and turbulent episodes in Arab history. A shortcut, to repeat one of Charles Issawi's pungent aphorisms, is not only the longest distance between two points; it is quite often the most perilous route.[50]

NOTES

1 Fernand Braudel, *The Perspective of the World*, Vol. 3 (New York: Harper & Row, 1979), p. 621.

2 See, for example, Robert Lauer, *Perspectives on Social Change* (Boston: Allyn & Bacon, Inc., 1982); Irene Gendzier, *Managing Political Change: Social Scientists and the Third World* (Boulder, Col.: Westview Press, 1985).

3 Samir Khalaf, *Lebanon's Predicament* (New York: Columbia University Press, 1986).

4 Of the many criticisms of the earlier paradigms, particularly the tradition-modernity dichotomy, the following are worth noting: David Apter, "The Role of Traditionalism in the Political Modernization of Ghana and Uganda," in David Apter, ed., *Some Conceptual Approaches to the Study of Modernization* (Englewood Cliffs, N.J.: Prentice Hall, Inc., 1968), pp. 133–5; Reinhard Bendix, "Tradition and Modernity Reconsidered," *Comparative Studies in Society and History*, 9 (April 1967), 292–346; S. N. Eisenstadt, "Studies of Modernization and Sociological Theory," *History and Theory*, 13, no. 3 (1974), 225–52; idem, "Reflections on a Theory of Modernization, in A. Rivkin, ed., *Nations by Design* (New York: Anchor Books, 1968), pp. 35–61; André G. Frank, *Sociology of Development and Underdevelopment of Sociology* (London: Pluto Press, 1971); B. F. Hozelitz, "Tradition and Economic Growth," in R. Braibanti and J. Z. Spengler, eds., *Traditions, Values and Economic Development* (Durham: Duke University Press, 1961), pp. 83–113; Marion J. Levy, Jr., "Contrasting Factors in the Modernization of China and Japan," *Economic Development and Cultural Change*, 2 (1953/4), 161–97; Ali Mazrui, "From Social Darwinism to Current Theories of Modernization," *World Politics* 21 (October 1968), 68–83; Fred G. Riggs, *Administration in Developing Countries: The Theory of Prismatic Society* (Boston: Houghton Mifflin, 1964); Edward Shils, "Tradition," *Comparative Studies in Society and History*, 13 (1971), 122–59; Dean C. Tipps, "Modernization Theory and the Comparative Study of Societies: A Critical Perspective," *Comparative Studies in Society and History*, 15 (March 1973), 199–226.

And the following papers in A. R. Desai, ed., *Essays on Modernization of Underdeveloped Societies*, vol. 1 (Bombay: Thacker & Co.,

Ltd, 1971); A. R. Desai, "Need for Revaluation of the Concept," pp. 474–548; Gail Omvedt, "Modernization Theories: The Ideology of Empire," pp. 119–27; M. N. Srinivas, "Modernization: A Few Queries," pp. 138–48; R. Sinai, "Modernization and the Poverty of Social Science," pp. 53–75; W. F. Wertheim, "The Way Towards 'Modernity,'" pp. 76–94.

5 Bendix, "Tradition and Modernity Reconsidered."
6 John Lewis, "The Social Limits of Politically Induced Change," in Chandler Morse et al., eds., *Modernization by Design* (Ithaca and London: Cornell University Press, 1969), p. 4.
7 Ibid., pp. 6, 10.
8 Clifford Geertz, *Agricultural Involution: The Process of Ecological Change in Indonesia* (Berkeley: University of California Press, 1968), p. 81.
9 Ibid., p. 103.
10 Khalaf, *Lebanon's Predicament.*
11 Ernest Gellner and J. Waterbury, eds., *Patrons and Clients in Mediterranean Societies* (London: Duckworth, 1977).
12 D. Eickelman, *The Middle East: An Anthropological Approach* (Englewood Cliffs, N.J.: Prentice Hall, Inc., 1981).
13 Dankward Rustow and Robert Ward, *Political Modernization in Japan and Turkey* (Princeton: Princeton University Press, 1964), p. 445.
14 Ibid.
15 For further details, see S. N. Eisenstadt, *Traditional Patrimonialism and Modern Neopatrimonialism* (Beverly Hills, Calif.: Sage, 1973).
16 Eisenstadt, "Studies of Modernization and Sociological Theory," p. 241.
17 Gellner, "Post-Traditional Forms in Islam."
18 Ibid., p. 206.
19 James Bill and Carl Leiden, *Politics in the Middle East* (2nd ed.; Boston: Little, Brown & Co., 1984), pp. 74–131.
20 J. Nash, J. Dandler, and N. Hopkins, eds., *Popular Participation in Social Change* (The Hague: Mouton Publishers, 1976).
21 Michael Cernea, "Modernization and Development Potential of Traditional Grass Roots Peasant Organizations," in M. Attir, B. Holzner, and Z. Suda, eds., *Directions of Change Modernization Theory, Research and Realities* (Boulder, Col.: Westview Press, 1981), p. 130.
22 Ibid.
23 N. J. Colletta, "The Use of Indigenous Culture as a Medium for Development: The Indonesian Case," *Prisma*, 1 (November 1975), 62.
24 Elizabeth Warnock Fernea, *Women and the Family in the Middle East* (Austin: University of Texas Press, 1985).
25 See, among others, Daniel Lerner, *The Passing of Traditional Society* (Glencoe, Ill.: The Free Press, 1982).
26 For added substantiation of the notion that traditional institutions may

be adaptive to modern society and politics, see Joseph Gusfield, "Tradition and Modernity: Misplaced Polarities in the Study of Social Change," *American Journal of Sociology*, 72 (January 1967), 351–62; Milton Singer, *When a Great Tradition Modernizes* (New York: Praeger Publishers, 1972); Ann Willner, "The Undeveloped Study of Political Development," *World Politics*, 16 (April 1964), 468–82; Robert N. Bellah, "Continuity and Change in Japanese Society," in B. Barber and A. Inkeles, eds., *Stability and Change* (Boston: Little, Brown & Co., 1971), pp. 377–404.

27 For a discussion of the meaning and tension between essentialism and apochalism, see Clifford Geertz, "After the Revolution: The Fate of Nationalism in the New States," in Barber and Inkeles, *Stability and Change*, pp. 357–76.

28 S. N. Eisenstadt, among others, has in several of his earlier writings emphasized the discontinuities and breakdowns inherent in the process of modernization. See his "Breakdowns of Modernization," *Economic Development and Cultural Change*, 12 (July 1964), 345–67; and his *Modernization: Protest and Change* (Englewood Cliffs, N.J.: Prentice-Hall, 1966).

29 Samuel P. Huntington, "The Political Modernization of Traditional Monarchies," *Daedalus*, 39 (Summer 1966), 766.

30 Charles Issawi, *An Economic History of the Middle of the Middle East and North Africa* (New York: Columbia University Press, 1982), p. 227.

31 C. E. Welch, "The Comparative Study of Political Modernization," in C. E. Welch, ed., *Political Modernization* (Belmond, Calif.: Wadsworth Publishing Co., 1967).

32 See Khalaf, *Lebanon's Predicament*, for further details.

33 See Janet Abu Lughod, "Migrant Adjustment to City Life: The Egyptian Case,0" *American Journal of Sociology*, 67 (July 1961), 22–32; Michael Bonine, "Urban Studies in the Middle East," *Middle East Studies Association Bulletin*, 10 (October 1976), 1–37; John Gulick, *Tripoli: A Modern Arab City* (Cambridge, Mass.: Harvard University Press, 1967); Samir Khalaf and Per Kongstad, *Hamira of Beirut: A Case of Rapid Urbanization* (Leiden: E. J. Brill, 1973).

34 Gellner and Waterbury, *Patrons and Clients in Mediterranean Societies*.

35 Emile Durkheim, *The Division of Labor in Society* (Glencoe, Ill.: The Free Press, 1964), p. 14.

36 A notable exception in this regard is Samuel Huntington; see his *Political Order in Changing Societies* (New Haven: Yale University Press, 1968).

37 For a clarification of this point see Robert A. Nisbet, *The Sociological Tradition* (New York: Basic Books, 1967), pp. 132–41. This conception comes close to the sacred collectivity model outlined in David Apter, *The Politics of Modernization* (Chicago: University of Chicago Press, 1965), pp. 31–3.

38 For an elaboration of this viewpoint see Chandler Morse, "Becoming vs. Being Modern: An Essay on Institutional Change and Economic Development," in Morse et al., *Modernization by Design*, pp. 238–382.

39 Durkheim, *Division of Labor in Society*, p. 28.

40 Lerner, *The Passing of Traditional Society;* Edward Shils, *Political Development in the New States* (The Hague: Mouton & Co., 1962); Manfred Halpern, *The Politics of Social Change in the Middle East and North Africa* (Princeton: Princeton University Press, 1963); Karl Deutsch, "Social Mobilization and Political Development," *American Political Science Review*, 55 (September 1961), 493–514; Eisenstadt, *Modernization: Protest and Change*.

41 P. Berger, B. Berger, and H. Kellner, *The Homeless Mind* (New York: Random House, 1973), pp. 119–38.

42 Magdi Hassanain, *The Sahara: Revolution and Promise: The Story of Tahrir Province* (in Arabic) (Cairo: General Book Organization, 1975).

43 John Waterbury, *The Egypt of Nasser and Sadat* (Princeton: Princeton University Press, 1983), p. 297.

44 Willard Beling, *Pan-Arabism and Labor* (Cambridge, Mass.: Harvard University Press, 1960).

45 Donald Warwick, *Bitter Pills: Population Policies and Their Implementation in Eight Developing Countries* (Cambridge and New York: Cambridge University Press, 1982).

46 L. Carl Brown, ed., *From Medina to Metropolis* (Princeton: The Darwin Press, 1973); Ellen Micaud, "Urbanization, Urbanism, and the Medina in Tunis," *International Journal of Middle East Studies*, 9 (November 1978), 431–47; Eickelman, *The Middle East: An Anthropological Approach*.

47 Deutsch, "Social Mobilization and Political Development," p. 464.

48 Alex Inkeles, "The Modernization of Man," in Myron Weiner, ed., *Modernization: Dynamics of Growth* (New York: Basic Books, 1966), p. 151–66.

49 Ernest Gellner, "Forward," in Said Arjomand, ed., *From Nationalism to Revolutionary Islam* (London: The Macmillan Press Ltd., 1984), p. vii.

50 Charles Issawi, *Issawi's Laws of Social Motion* (New York: Hawthorn Books, 1973), p. 8.

6 · Women and social change*

AFAF LUTFI AL-SAYYID-MARSOT
University of California, Los Angeles

In an article entitled "Orientalism and Arab Women," Rosemary Sayigh stated what she described as an obvious fact: that women are members of groups and share the same influences that modify such groups as a whole; but the group allocates to women functions as women within that group, so that external forces reach them via their position as women within the family and class structure. Yet women are themselves actors, and it is the interaction between them and their society that is important for us.[1] We would do well to keep these facts in mind. I have no desire to reify women's studies, still less do I intend to lump Arab women together as one entity, which clearly they are not. But I would like to discuss some aspects of social change that have taken place in the last decades in the Arab world.

In a recent television program a play opens with a husband and wife quarreling in an upper-middle-class drawing room. The husband turns to his wife, snarling, "I own you." Does this scene take place in the Middle East? No; it is in England, between the two world wars. At whatever period in time, regardless of geographic location, strong family systems tend to develop systems of control over females. The condition of women within their society is thus a function of historical experience, economic situation, class affiliation, degree of education, and so on. Hence Arab women differ from one another not only in time and space but also within the same country and along class lines.

The relationship between the sexes over time has undergone various changes, none of which seems to take place in a linear fashion but rather in a cyclical one, with gains on the one hand measured against losses on the other. I would like to concentrate on three aspects of change in women's lives: sexual, economic, and social in the general sense. These aspects, to my mind, form different views of looking at the same phenomenon.

Frequently, the relationships between the sexes in Muslim societies have been attributed to religion. The segregation of women and the veil are said to arise from the dictates of the Quran, so that many Muslims and non-Muslims believe that Islam has created a distinctive social structure, one that is gelled in time and is believed to represent "the Muslim way of life," or Muslim society par excellence. Talal Asad, in a brilliant essay, points out the misapprehensions of such a stand.[2] He states that Islam is a tradition consisting of discourses which seek to instruct practitioners, and that, as with all instituted practices, it is oriented to a concept of the past and the future through a present, Orthodoxy, crucial to tradition, is a relationship of power. Argument and conflict over the form and significance of practices are natural to any tradition and do not represent "crisis." Consequently, traditions should not be regarded as essentially homogeneous: "The variety of traditional Islamic practices in different times, places, and populations indicates the different Islamic reasonings that different social and historical conditions can or cannot sustain." We thus seek to understand the historical conditions that develop or transform traditions and the efforts of practitioners to achieve coherence. The relationship between the sexes can then be understood as a relationship of power, which is constantly changing, as all such relationships are, and which is in some measure tied to the past, to history. Such relationships are not homogeneous and are subject to the same forces that impinge on any other society.

In most works about women written in the past by men of the Arab world or by researchers outside the Arab world, there seems to be an emphasis on the notion that Muslim men believe women to have a rampant sexuality, which must be kept in check by careful supervision. One might be tempted to dismiss this notion as deriving from a feverish orientalist imagination, which actually tells us more about the sexual problems of the author – except for the fact that this view is also shared by Muslim/Arab men. Because of this alleged sexuality, which diverts men from their religious and political duties, women are viewed as a force for chaos and a social danger. Hence they must be controlled, and one form of control is the veil – and here I use the term loosely to mean anything from a head covering to seclusion in a harem.

A word of warning, however: the veil is a culture-specific way of dressing and in itself has no significance except as a response to certain weather conditions, such as sun and dust.[3] What sets the veil apart are the connotations behind it. Passages in the Quran have been adduced as justification for the veil and the segregation of women, for example, Sura 24:31, "They [the believing women] shall cover their breasts with their veils" (*wal-yadribna bi-khumuri-hina ʿala juyubihina*); and Sura 33:59, where women are enjoined "to lengthen their garments" (*Yudnina ʿalayhina min jalabibihina*) when leaving the house. Another passage, Sura 4:34, which states that "men are the providers for women," although some would translate it as "managers of the affairs of women" (*al-rijalu qawa-muna ʿala al-nisaiʾ*), was transformed into a belief that men are the guardians of women. Changing socioeconomic conditions caused these and other Quranic passages to become interpreted in a way that encouraged the segregation of women. Covering the breasts and lengthening the outer garment became transformed into an injunction to cover the entire body, except for hands and feet, and in some areas to cover the face as well. The next step was to segregate women, and to interpret the Quranic passage where men are said to be the providers for women into a belief that men are guardians over women, since women are segregated. Gradually women were demoted to the level of children or mental incompetents who require guardians.

Yet segregation was contrary to the spirit of the numerous passages in the Quran which stress the equality of the sexes by stating that men and women are equal parts of a pair (*zawj*), both having the same appetites and needs. There is not the slightest hint that women are oversexed and dangerous. As portrayed in the Quran Eve is not even the temptress: it is Adam who is tempted by the serpent.[4] How, then, have men developed the notion of an unbridled female sexuality?

To seek a partial answer to this question we might go to the realm of psychology rather than that of religion, for the notion of the oversexed female is not unique to the Arab world but is found in Latin and Mediterranean countries as well; it is, in fact, allegedly present in the psychological makeup of all males. Psychoanalysts believe that male children, in the phallic stage of development, suffer from a castration complex. Because the first object in the life of the child is the mother, castration anxiety leads to the renunciation of that illicit attraction, resulting in a split image of the female as both goddess/mother and seductress/prostitute, and creating fears regarding the *vagina dentata*.[5] Consequently, the "demanding female" becomes nothing more than the projection of a male sexual fantasy or of a male fear of inadequacy in the face of a creature of fantasy. Fears of castration or of inadequacy, added to socialization, are transformed into an overwhelming machismo, manifested by a preoccupation with the purity of the females in one's group, a desire to prove one's manhood (which often results in a Don Juan complex), and a concomitant belief that women are insatiable sexual beings. Women are believed to exert such a powerful sexual aura that even looking at them is sufficient to arouse the male and distract him from his duties. Thus they must be segregated. When al-Ghazali said in justification of the segregation of women, "The look is the fornication of the eye," he was referring to scoptophilia or the sexualization of the sensation of looking, a partial instinct found in all male children.[6] The conclusions derived from such beliefs were that decent God-fearing men should restrain female sexuality by keeping women in ignorance of it, ashamed of it, under wraps, and away from temptation. The Puritans did it one way, the Muslims another, because of different socioeconomic conditions and a different historical experience.

Thus woman has become an eternal sleeping beauty who must not be awakened, and man has developed a double standard of morality in order to satisfy his own sexual needs. Men seek pleasure with loose women, that is women who can be bought, public women to whom one is not accountable for satisfaction (a duty incumbent on every husband, according to the Quran), and who are there to be used (although that is a sin in the Quran); and they marry "pure" women, who are kept ignorant of their own sexuality and of the outside world. In some eras of the past, education was viewed as corrupting women's morals. Some men went so far as to say that women lacked mind and religion (*'aql wa din*); therefore it was better to leave them unlettered for they might be tempted to read about their sexual natures and seek to find out more. Lest the eyes of women be opened, then it was preferable to segregate them, and even to perform clitoridectomy. There is, no doubt, a world of difference between veiling, segregation, and clitoridectomy, but they are all symbols of male domination over women and of women's seclusion from society.

Historically, seclusion of women was not limited to the Arab world but was practiced by a number of societies, the Byzantine and the Sassanian, to name but two who introduced the Arabs to that custom. But we need to go from the general sexual-psychological reasons for controlling women, which exist in all societies, to more specific socioeconomic reasons that express the manner in which a particular society handles gender relationships. There are other reasons for keeping women dominated by men, which any article on feminism will provide; but I have chosen to concentrate on certain aspects – the sexual, the economic, and the social – given the limitations of space.

In addition to men's desire to control and dominate, keeping women isolated from society allows property to fall under male control; furthermore, segregation prevents women from competing in the marketplace. The Muslim law of inheritance specifies the right of women to inherit from parents, spouses, siblings, and offspring. A legal (*halal*) way of sidestepping that law was to isolate women, especially rich women, which theoretically would render them economically ineffective and dependent upon men. While this was undoubtedly a deterrent, it was not always effective, and we find at certain periods in history that harem women in the Ottoman capital and in Cairo, to name but two examples, wheeled and dealed with the best of them. Throughout the seventeenth and eighteenth centuries, in some Muslim countries, women of all classes shared in the economic life of the country by owning land, buying and selling property, and engaging in trade and commerce. The end of the eighteenth century and the beginning of the nineteenth saw the incorporation of the Arab world into the world market. With the advent of a cash-crop economy and imported manufactured goods, which eventually subverted cottage industries, women became marginalized in economic terms. Even women of the elite who inherited property according to the dictates of the *sharia* seem to have turned over the management of their property to men. It is likely that women either were unable to deal with an alien world market or were forced out of it by men. The reasons for the economic marginalization of women may lie elsewhere than in the world market, but my recent research shows that women had an active economic role in the eighteenth century which they lost in the nineteenth, and which they are slowly and unevenly beginning to reclaim in the latter part of the twentieth century.

An illegal but often adopted way of sidestepping the law of inheritance in the past was simply to cut women out of an inheritance. This was generally the case within many Muslim rural communities up to the fairly recent past, but since labor was scarce in most agricultural areas (except for Egypt in the twentieth century), women worked alongside men. Consequently, the strictures regarding isolation and veiling, which were rigidly applied to elite urban women, were only rarely applied to rural women, for example, only to the wives of the ʿumdas. Following the example of the urban elite, the ʿumdas kept their wives segregated to show that they were affluent, did not need to put their wives to work, and, indeed, could afford to provide their wives with servants.

It may well be that a belief in the power of female sexuality, when added to economic motivation, created an ideology that sought to dominate and segregate women. This ideology was originally grounded in the urban milieu and among the bourgeoisie, and then trickled down to the rural milieu. There, instead of being segregated (which would have made little economic sense), women worked and occupied an important space in the marketplace until the nineteenth century; they subscribed, however, to the same code of morality, made somewhat less rigid by economic necessity.

Thus we find among urban and rural populations a similar ideology regarding the need to segregate men and women, especially in countries with highly homogeneous societies, such as Egypt, although there the practice differed in that the elite urban women and the women of the bourgeoisie were segregated up to the twentieth century, but rural women were not, and neither were working-class urban women, as we have shown.

Similar attitudes regarding the need to dominate women exist to the present day in a somewhat attenuated or even different form, arising from the socioeconomic conditions of the times. The trend towards the domination of women can be seen clearly in certain social aspects, for example in the realm of education. In some Arab societies women are generally permitted an education of sorts, that is, one which is more suited to their "femininity" – whatever that may mean. In others they receive a more or less equal education.

In an article in *Sharq al-Awsat* (1 February 1984) Dr. Ibrahim al-Salqini, dean of the College of Sharia at Damascus University, was quoted as saying, "We cannot deny that a woman is capable of understanding the same things as a man, but she must study what is suitable for her nature, and that which prepares her for her great task, which is more important than raising nuclear power stations: that of raising future generations." He added, "Women may be trained to become nurses, social workers, teachers and doctors to serve their own sex, but as to their studying chemistry, engineering, and like matters, these will detract from the basic duty for which a woman was created." Another man, expert in *sharia*, quoted in another issue (7 May 1984) of the same newspaper, when asked whether Muslim women are entitled to work outside the home, answered: "So long as the woman is not laid open to degradation or to insult, for God has wanted for her nothing but protection and honor or respect" – the implication being that a woman in the marketplace is bound to be degraded and insulted. But if a woman, why not a man? If not, why not? And is not poverty or dependence even more degrading?

Once again, the answer would seem to lie in the notion of sexuality, the belief that ineluctably women will attract men and so leave themselves open to insult. It would seem as though no relationship other than the sexual is possible between men and women, unless it be the veneration of the mother. I hope I am not putting words into the mouth of our *sharia* expert, but that is the one interpretation that springs to mind, especially when he adds that women are capable of doing all that a man can do, but that their jobs should be limited to those "which fit their natures," and to the task of "breeding and raising future generations."

I can say in all seriousness that these views represent a great advance over the views of past generations. At least these gentlemen do not think that women lack the brainpower to study science, as some men did in the past; but they simply cannot see beyond the sexuality and reproductive function of women.

Many women, for a variety of reasons, go along with the belief that they must be guided and protected by males. Whether they have accepted the male philosophy, or are too insecure in matters of religion to argue with the "learned men", or whether it is the path of safest action and least resistance is debatable. As a consequence of early societal conditioning women perpetuate the same myths concerning male superiority and female need for protection. Some recent laws concerning divorce, regarded as progressive, are in fact based on the notion of the weakness of the female and the need to protect her as befits her function of mother. For example, the Egyptian laws which allow a woman to keep her dwelling after a divorce are predicated on the notion that she will have custody of her children and will need a home for them.[7] No Arab woman in her right senses would consider giving up custody of her children, save in cases of the most extreme kind; and no judge would grant custody to the father unless the mother was proved to have loose morals or was declared insane. It is only fair, the reasoning goes, since the woman is not equipped to earn a living, that she be supported by the man in return for her services as wife and mother; after a divorce she should at least retain the conjugal abode in order to care for her young. Once she is divorced, however, financial support from her husband soon comes to an end and she must rely on another male relative. In times of financial necessity, as in the present time among non-oil producing countries, such a condition becomes even more onerous than in the past, when extended families were the norm. Hence the current move to educate women, so that they can earn a living if they have to. Yet by so doing, women would be competing for the same employment as men, a paradox. So how does a society make women less of a burden and at the same time take them out of the competition?

This accounts in part for the ambivalent attitude found in the Arab world and elsewhere toward the education of women and their training for a profession, as well as to their going out to work and earning a living. The answer, according to some men, is to educate women to serve other women or to take on the jobs that men do not want.

Interestingly, it is those countries in the Arab world that are among the richest which hold the most protective attitudes towards women, while the poorer countries seem to be more ambivalent, although this was not necessarily the case in the past. For example in Egypt, Jordan, and Iraq women have been out in the marketplace for some time. There are more women in the Egyptian National Assembly than in the United States Congress, and several Egyptian cabinet ministers have been women. This tells us that there is a group of Muslim-Arab women occupying positions in public life that theoretically belong to the male-dominated domains.[8] Here we might look closer to determine whether such a "liberated attitude" is typical of all the women in Egypt; or, if not, is it typical of a social class?

It is quite clear that in Egypt, for example, emancipation spread first among women of the upper bourgeoisie, for they had a choice of working or not and were not constrained to work out of necessity, as were women of the poorer classes. Yet when we look at professional women in general, we find that they come from all classes – no one class has a monopoly of working women. It is equally clear that women from the lower social echelons work out of economic necessity and make up the lower ranks of the work force. They occupy the lowest paid jobs: they are schoolteachers, minor bureaucrats, nurses, and so on; while bourgeois women generally, though not exclusively, go into the professions in larger numbers. Perhaps because their economic needs are not as acute they can afford the luxury of delaying their earning capabilities by going to a university; perhaps knowing that their future jobs as professionals will be better paid is the incentive.

Women of the bourgeoisie – in Egypt, Jordan, Iraq, Tunisia, and so on – the most modernized of women, do not look to justify their attending a university or seeking a job. They do it as a matter of course. Their battles were fought for them by a past generation of women. Struggling to assert their emancipation as part of the politi-

cal revolution that began in Egypt, women removed the veil in 1920.
This action was later imitated by Syrian, Iraqi, and Jordanian
women, for Egypt was, up to the 1970s, the social and political
leader of the Arab world.[9] Should we desire to be more specific, we
would have to say that women who came from affluent, urban, and
educated backgrounds in Egypt and the Fertile Crescent were the
first to become emancipated because they had an economic choice.
Here I will stick my neck out (and I am ready to see it chopped off!)
and say that in many instances the encouragement these women
received to emancipate themselves came from their fathers, and not
from their mothers. Perhaps because men had suffered by marrying
ignorant women, they wanted their daughters to become educated.
Once educated, it was difficult to deny these women a public position as well. Some fathers may have been more enlightened –
whatever that means – or because they were affluent they did not
fear economic competition from women. Or perhaps they wanted
to show that they were "westernized" or "modernized." The
mothers, on the other hand, were more interested in seeing their
daughters well married with their future prosperity assured.

There are, of course, exceptions, and since no one has made a
survey of working women and asked about the source of inspiration
in their lives, I conclude from the little I know that it is the men who
moved towards emancipating their daughters. The early male supporters of feminism gave as a justification their belief that keeping
half of a society in ignorance was damaging to the national cause;
others adduced religious reasons, saying that God had created man
and woman to be equal in all things, including intelligence, and that
an educated woman could raise better-educated children than an
ignorant woman could. One must keep in mind that these men were
thinking in nationalist terms and were trying to impress a colonial
power with their progressive attitudes in the hope of being granted
independence. It was a common ploy of the colonial powers to point
to the condition of Muslim women as an example of "ignorance,"
and to justify their continued presence as part of the function of
"educating" or "civilizing" the colonized.

When we examine the lower-middle and lower classes today we
find different attitudes. The men of the petty bourgeoisie are themselves preoccupied with problems of earning a living and would
rather keep women out of the market and out of the competition for
the limited jobs available. Many working men complain that
women take jobs away from them because they are willing to work
in factories for lower wages and do not respect union orders (e.g.,

they will not strike).[10] (This is almost a parody of the situation after World War II, when returning GIs asked Rosie the Riveter and her counterparts to go back home and produce babies instead of taking work away from deserving males.) Therefore, working men today would rather that women did not work. At the same time, with rising inflation and rising expectations there is the felt need for a two-salary family. So reluctantly, men allow their daughters to work until marriage, or allow their wives to go on working until the mythical day when they can afford to forego a second salary.[11] The dilemma these men face, however, is how to protect women from other men when they are in the marketplace. Given the male belief in the oversexed female, how can men ensure that women remain pure and untouched? Over the past decade this dilemma has been resolved, probably by working women themselves: they have sought to develop their own identity within their own culture by a return to the veil. By inventing a more modest attire patterned after the dress of a nun, these women have followed the injunction in Suras al-Ahzab and al-Nur, but have interpreted it in the strictest sense with regard to modesty of attire, making it overwhelmingly modest. This allows them to earn a living but at the same time issues a signal that *this* woman is not to be harassed. Hence the existence of "Muslim dress," which has little Islamic about it save the signal it sends out, namely, that the woman is not receptive to being sexually approached. Until attitudes towards working women change such a distinctive attire will be regarded as a shield and a protection.

Urban middle-class women may not face the same urgency for earning their keep as working-class women; but since the middle class is the one that has recently suffered the most from a diminishing standard of living, the need for women to seek jobs is even more acute if they are to maintain their status within society. As the middle class takes its signals, albeit diluted, from the upper class, the women are also educated and allowed to work until they marry. Then, depending on the economic needs of the married couple, the women either continue to work or stay home to rear the children. Education is seen as an economic asset, for if women do not work they can at least teach the children. Given the low standards of schooling in most of the Middle East, the mother takes on the duty of schoolteacher, and by so doing lessens the need for expensive private tutorials – the norm in countries like Egypt. The idea here is to keep the woman at home, but to keep her busy and useful by teaching the children.

As for the rural married woman, she works all of her life and has enough trouble keeping body and soul together without busying herself with problems of emancipation. Rural women have managed to secure a share of the marketplace through their entrepreneurial talents, for example, in making cheese and butter, and raising poultry and livestock. In some Arab countries women go to the weekly market to barter and sell their wares, and so actively participate in the family economy. In other countries women control their own resources, in still others all goes to the husband, and if and when a wife gets her share it is by manipulation or guile. Recent studies of the "new Arab social order" show that there is a reversal to a *status quo ante* on the part of rural women, for as their husbands emigrate to oil-rich countries wives are forced to take on the job of working the land, especially in Syria and in Egypt.

Recent studies also show that the informal market is thriving and more affluent than some segments of the formal market,[12] and it is here that the talents of women shine. Women sell garden produce, fruit, trinkets, even smuggled items. More affluent urban women sell clothes, both new (imported from abroad) and old, and beauty products to their friends, make dresses, or become caterers – all of which is done informally, without the expense of a government license or the burden of paying taxes. Oddly enough, in some countries – and here I again use Egypt as the example – women are also involved in the illegal market. A few are notorious in the drug trade, or in controlling groups of toughs who will beat up an opponent, ruin a wedding, or vandalize a shop for a price; or they may control crews of beggars, gangs of thieves, or prostitution rings. In the legal market women have also taken on certain trades that are most "macho." There are women taxi drivers and coffee house owners as well as women butchers, who in the abattoirs are often more feared than men. Whether this is true in other Arab countries is unknown to me, but there is little reason to assume otherwise.

Economically, then, an exiguous but growing number of women in certain Arab countries today are fully emancipated when it comes to earning a living in some domain previously monopolized by men, such as medicine, engineering, politics, contracting, import and export, and so on. Although their numbers are small, the fact that they are there at all is significant.[13]

There is a definite attempt to bring women into the marketplace, especially in Syria, Iraq, and Jordan. Clearly, the governments of these countries see the need for the man- (or is it the person-?) power generated by women, and laws are passed to help qualify women for work. Other countries see little need for involving women in the work force, or even for involving some of the men, since they have a lot of oil money and can import labor. With the fall in the price of oil worldwide, we may see a new trend developing. And yet the women in those countries have found a way of becoming part of the economic life. In the example of Saudi women we find a separate but parallel economic world that is dominated by women and run by women for women. The rise of a bank catering to women or businesses run by women catering to the needs of women are examples. In some feminist circles in the United States this type of parallel but separate activity of the sexes has been hailed as a great triumph of feminism, and even of emancipation.

The third aspect of change for women that I want to consider, aside from the sexual and the economic, lies in the social realm. It is true that sexuality and economic roles are also social aspects, but I believe we can talk about a purely social aspect that encompasses all other elements such as economics, politics, religion, and human relations. Here we might pause a minute and underline three important points made by Rosemary Sayigh.[14] First, women's social roles are stronger than those of men, for women are what holds a society together. They are the forces of socialization, the guardians of tradition, popular lore, and community history. They communicate news, offer help and advice to others, and develop the national consciousness. Second, families are social units and part of the political and economic nexus of a country, and thus are affected by the external policies and the political requirements of the times. Third, even though secluded women still have extra-domestic functions which may not necessarily be apparent to the outsider, they engage in parapolitical actions such as peacemaking or sustaining community feeling between warring factions, and they participate in protest movements and revolutions.

One group that seems most preoccupied with all matters pertaining to women, education, economic roles, and so forth is the *ulama*, who claim to set the norms for "legitimate" behavior. In recent years there has been a plethora of newspaper articles about women's dress, their right to work, education, and so on, supported in most Arab countries by the absolutist governments of the day (exceptions being Syria and Iraq). This ties in with the rise of *jamaat* and of fundamentalist movements. Beginning with Sadat, religious organizations in Egypt have been encouraged to come forward as valid interlocutors in political and social matters. Because the Muslim Brothers were opponents of Nasserism (the ideology that Sadat hoped to displace), his government assumed religious organizations would be natural allies. At the same time, the increasing preoccupation with religious matters was to keep the population busied and deflect attention from political matters, especially foreign affairs. Religion was to be manipulated or used as a smoke screen in politicoeconomic terms, but it became a genuine issue in socioeconomic terms. What the administration planned as a role for religion and what the populace planned for the role of religion were two different things. The battleground can be clearly seen in the issues affecting women.

Many of the articles dealing with the resurgence of Islam in Egypt trace it to the events in 1967 and the defeat.[15] There was a palpable shift in mood towards matters of religion in an attempt to answer the question: "What went wrong? Why were the Arabs defeated?" The obvious answer, one dealing with leadership and military capabilities as well as autocratic governments, was too drastic and would require dramatic changes in government, which the average citizen would be unable to carry out. The alternative, then, was to resort to talk of spiritual shortcomings, a line the leaders of the day encouraged. It was far preferable for the authorities to blame defeat on the people's departure from religious norms rather than on their own military and political ineptness. The population was willing to take the rap, so to speak, because behind such a notion lay a subtle hint of revolution. For if the people had strayed from religious norms, then clearly so had their leaders, who must perforce reform themselves or accept their own loss of legitimacy. And in Muslim terminology a leader without legitimacy must be overthrown.

Religious resurgence gained momentum under Sadat and continued to grow, especially with the Open Door policy. That policy led to inflation, rampant consumerism, and increasing gaps between rich and poor; it also resulted in a new ethos that stressed the individual and his wants to the detriment of the rest of his society; a "me generation" had come into existence. In Egypt, Syria, and Iraq religious movement grew for different reasons, but they all had in common the notions that there were no channels of communication with the authorities, that man had become irrelevant in the eyes of the administration, which worked to satisfy a small elite and turned a deaf ear to the masses. Because the governments were too powerful, civil disobedience was ruled out for the time being, save in isolated instances of violence or terrorism, and the mosque became the meeting place for opposition. Religious resurgence, which was the outcome of spiritual and physical distress, became wedded to political action and opposition to the governments of the day.

Whether *jamaat* in Egypt, *Ikhwan* in Syria, or *Da^cwa Islamiyya* in Iraq, the basic premise was that reform could occur only with a return to the Muslim ways of life. In brief, Muslim ways of life became a shorthand idiom for several important politicoeconomic changes: (1) a redistribution of wealth in the form of *zakat*, which aside from charity posits a yearly distribution of 2.5% of capital gains for the needy; (2) a government of laws, not of whim or caprice of the strong man in power; and (3) consultation or *shura*, which would bring into power groups other than the elite of a sect, a village, or a family. The religious movement was clearly an economic and political movement as well.

From the outset, women were involved in the religious resurgence movement. It may well be that those who had lost a husband, son, or brother in the war turned to the Almighty for consolation, but it is also in part because women had to deal with the difficulties of household economy, inflation, and seeing men go off to work in oil-rich countries because they could not satisfy the demands of their families locally – a widespread phenomenon in Syria, Jordan, Yemen, Sudan, and elsewhere.[16] Women, then, were as discontented with their situation as men were. As the economic situation worsened, the poorer-class women felt constrained to go out and work. Women of the petty and middle bourgeoisie were unaccustomed to consorting freely with men in a work milieu, for they had led a more sheltered life than either the upper-class or the working women. Because they feared advances which they could not handle, they opted for "Muslim dress," which protected them from harassment. Upper-class women followed suit, as a protest against the present form of government and the consumer mentality, believing that outward attire made a stronger statement than words could. Yet other women, cynically seeking to protect their newfound wealth and position from criticism or attack, hid behind the new garb as though by so doing they could deny the exploitative origins of their wealth. Islamic attire soon became a fashion, and women who were neither overtly religious nor had a political statement to make opted to dress in that way to be like all the others. It may be recalled that the Muslim style of clothing has obvious advantages: it does not have to follow the latest and often expensive fashion, thus it is a money saver; it prevents women who wish to acquire an education and to work from being taken for loose women, for it shows that they believe in traditional virtues and are not "westernized" – indeed, it is generally a sign of rejection of Western social values as being insufficient or unable to solve local problems.

The *ulama* and the leaders of the *jamaat* encouraged the wearing of such modest attire and adduced the passage from Sura al-Nur, claiming that the passage meant that women were to cover their shoulder bones, hence the neck as well. Soon women were wearing wimples in accord with that interpretation. Many an emancipated woman saw her daughter turn to Islamic garb with something akin to bewilderment, the more so because her own mother had struggled to remove the veil in her generation. Younger professional and working women believed they were making a statement by their style of clothing, and believed equally that the style conformed to the Muslim norms of dress. A debate, hotly contested by supporters of the style of dress and those against it, broke out in the press. The debate was exacerbated with the assassination of Sadat by members of one of the *jamaat*, which split Egypt into those sympathetic to the assassins and those horrified by the assassination.

Our interest, however, lies in the changing condition of women and why they have opted to dress differently. Some believe that a change of dress is irrelevant and simply a smoke screen designed to distract attention from the real issues facing the country, namely, its economic conditions and foreign policy; others tend to see Muslim garb as a symptom of social malaise, a reversal and a protest against trends followed by the government. I see it as a mixture of both, although for a long time I believed it was purely the latter. Now I can see how convenient it is for the authoritarian governments of the Arab world to involve people in irrelevant controversies of that sort. Apparently the position of women and the way they dress have become of interest to men as well as to women. Women's attire has become (1) a symbol of rejection of Western social values and life-styles (although not of Western technology), and of a return to cultural roots; (2) a sign of growing insecurity on the part of both sexes in the face of a rapidly changing society with which it is increasingly difficult to cope; and (3) a sign of economic competition between the sexes.

The *ulama*, who generally belong to the petty and middle bourgeoisie, by preaching the restriction of women are really protecting the interests of their own class and sex. Consequently, the issue of dress and of working women is sure to raise a debate wherever it is encountered, for political as well as for social and economic reasons. Those who would like Egypt to return to the Arab fold favor Islamic dress, for it shows to the more conservative regimes that Egypt is turning away from the West and towards Islamic tradition (even though these conservative regimes are becoming rapidly "modernized" and investing their petrobillions in the West). Those who are opposed to the government support the dress because it is an overt sign of dissidence. Those who are in economic need (and that includes the greater majority of the country) like the fact that it saves the headache of expenditure on dress. Those who are truly religious may be genuinely convinced that it is the sort of attire that is pleasing to God. The fact that the attire is a new fashion is irrelevant. Those in government who realize that their political and economic situation is precarious, or at least dicey, are pleased at something that gives the public grist for the mill and does not harm the administration. It saves having to blow up a town or hang a popular leader, as has been done in Syria and the Sudan as well as in Iraq – although violence cannot be controlled, as the Sadat assassination has shown.

While I have talked mainly about the situation in Egypt, the same conditions obtain in the other Arab countries, where fundamentalist movements are just as strong. In one sense even in their clothing styles women are being manipulated, as they have always been on many levels, for the defense or attack of fundamentalist movements is predicated on the women's outward appearance; it is also an example of how women are able to strike back and strike out on their own by opting for such attire. While being manipulated they also succeed in manipulating their society. Women who feel the economic necessity to work protect themselves from moral slurs cast at them by males by dressing differently, which in some ways allays male opposition. At the same time, the new social order that has come into existence in the region – the outcome of oil wealth in some countries and resulting labor migration from poor countries – has left many women without a husband or male relative. They may feel more vulnerable, more exposed to public censure, and they attempt to deflect that potential censure by adopting Muslim garb, simultaneously camouflaging their emancipation from many of the old restrictions. Necessity, absent males, or better paying positions abroad have forced women into taking on many responsibilities formerly reserved for men, such as paying the bills, investing money remitted, buying and selling, and so on.

In conclusion, what might seem as a regressive move on the part of women can in fact be interpreted as a progressive move leading toward more freedom for women rather than less. Obviously I am talking in general terms, and there are bound to be specific cases that contradict my statements. Time will show which interpretation is correct, but let us not make the mistake of assuming that dress is *necessarily* stating the obvious. The women who wears a bikini may not be the most emancipated, and neither is the woman wearing Muslim garb necessarily more or less religious than anyone else. Clothes do make a statement, but they make different statements depending on the social class of the wearer and the economic conditions of the country in which she lives.

There have been radical changes in the Arab world over the past decades, and we shall see even more radical changes in the near future. Whether or not women will benefit from them will depend on a number of variables. We can, however, count on the fact that changes are seldom linear, and what may appear to be an emancipatory move for women may in fact turn out to have disadvantageous economic consequences; but then, emancipation does not mean a better or a worse deal, it just means having the freedom to choose.

NOTES

* I am grateful to Dr. Jean-Louis Lerenard and to Ms. Sherry Vatter for their criticisms of an early draft of this paper, as I am to Ms. Garine Zetlian, my research assistant, for her help.
1 Rosemary Sayigh, "Orientalism and Arab Women," *Arab Studies Quarterly*, 3, no. 3 (1981), 266.
2 Talal Asad, *The Idea of an Anthropology of Islam*, Occasional Papers Series (Washington, D.C.: Georgetown University, 1986).
3 Nazih Ayubi, "Secularism and Modernization in Islam," *Free Inquiry*, 2 (Winter 1981), 18ff.
4 Jane Smith and Yvonne Haddad, "Eve: Islamic Image of Woman," in Azizah al-Hibri, ed., *Women and Islam* (New York: Pergamon, 1982).
5 Otto Fenichel, *The Psychoanalytic Theory of Neurosis* (New York: W. W. Norton and Co., 1945), pp. 71, 77–80.
6 Ibid., p. 79.
7 Egypt, Law No. 44, 1979, which has now been repealed.
8 See recent work by Earl L. Sullivan, *Women in Egyptian Public Life* (Syracuse: Syracuse University Press, 1986).
9 See articles in L. Beck and N. Keddie, eds., *Women in the Muslim World* (Cambridge, Mass.: Harvard University Press, 1978).
10 Mona Hammam, "Egypt's Working Women," *MERIP Report*, no. 82 (1981), 3 ff.
11 See Sawsan al-Messiri, "Self-Images of Traditional Urban Women in Cairo," in Beck and Keddie, pp. 522–40.
12 Barbara K. Larson, "The Structure and Function of Village Markets in

Contemporary Egypt," *Journal of the American Research Center in Egypt*, 19 (1982), 131ff.
13 Sullivan, *passim*.
14 These points were raised by Sayigh, pp. 269ff.
15 See special issue of the *International Journal of Middle East Studies*, 12, no. 4 (1980), especially articles by Saad Eddin Ibrahim, pp. 423–53, and by Nazih Ayubi, pp. 481–99.
16 Saad Eddin Ibrahim, "Oil, Migration and the New Arab Social Order, in M. Kerr and S. Yassin, eds., *Rich and Poor States in the Middle East* (Boulder, Col.: Westview Press, 1982), pp. 17ff.

7 · Knowledge and education in the modern Middle East: a comparative view

CARTER VAUGHN FINDLEY
Ohio State University

A brief survey of the state of knowledge and education in the Middle East of the nineteenth and twentieth centuries requires synthesizing at a high level of abstraction. Yet the undertaking appears justified by what it shows about important trends. To organize this inquiry, we may begin by postulating several basic points.

Since the only modern developments likely to flourish in Middle Eastern or other contexts are ones compatible with local traditions and structures, the first point is that traditional concepts of knowledge and patterns of knowledge diffusion exert a continuing influence. For example, the historical cultural elitism of the Middle East – with its obscure literary styles and low literacy rates, which cannot have stood much above 1% to 2% for the region in 1800 – still casts a long shadow. Also of continuing relevance are traditional concepts about the organization of knowledge. I shall follow Marshall Hodgson's view of the learned culture as being woven over time of four strands: the religious studies, with their rational concept of knowledge (*ilm*); mysticism (*tasawwuf*, centered on the gnostic concept of knowledge, *ma'rifa* or *irfan*); the worldly belletristic culture (*adab*); and the philosophical and natural-science strand (*falsafa*).[1] In commenting on intercivilizational transmission of knowledge, I shall emphasize the science-technology continuum, the domain of Western knowledge that is most difficult to acquire and of greatest current interest in the Middle East.

A second point, important for discussion of intercivilizational transmission of ideas, concerns the receptivity of Islamic civilization, as compared to others, to foreign ideas. Here we note that while the "strands" of the learned culture have displayed more or less openness to exogenous ideas at different times, *sharia* legal thought, in particular, tended to restrict borrowings, except in domains for which it offered few normative prescriptions.

130

A third point concerns social systems for support of education, science, and technology. There are more such topics than I can fully discuss. Are education and science more dependent on public initiative or private? Are these systems democratic or elitist in access, centralized or decentralized in organization? How high are levels of literacy or financial support? Are educators and scientists in agreement over the workings of the system, or divided by questions like cultural dualism or language of instruction?

Social factors that act immediately on education and science are part of a larger complex that may be described as the general constellation of conditions under which the world of knowledge evolves at any given time. These constellations we must take as a fourth theme. Nineteenth- and twentieth-century Middle Eastern history displays three such constellations – we cannot say three periods, as the constellations appear in different places at different dates, though in uniform sequence. The first constellation is that of European imperialism, direct or indirect, under which westernization and cultural dualism become central issues. The second is that of independence and mass mobilization under largely secular ideologies, whether liberal or populist-socialist in character. As the secularism of the ideologies implies, societies under this constellation display important continuities with those under the first. The third constellation is that of Islamic resurgence. The three sets of conditions are not mutually exclusive. Something of each appears under the others. Yet it is possible to talk of a set of conditions that is dominant or "in the ascendant" at a given time.

A survey of knowledge and education in the Middle East under the three constellations just defined, with reference to changes in the state of knowledge and in social systems for its production, will help to clarify the results of educational and scientific change over the last two centuries. In the concluding section, a comparison of the Middle East with other Asian centers of civilization will provide a measure of Middle Eastern achievement.

Knowledge and education under European dominance

In one way or another, European dominance continued throughout the nineteenth century and into the twentieth, not yielding to the Third World variety of independence until the 1920s in Turkey and Iran and after World War II for most of the Arab world. Implicitly, this was a period of possibilities, as indicated in Ibrahim Abu-Lughod's analogy between the nineteenth-century translation movement and that of the ninth century, which helped launch the literary and philosophical-scientific traditions of Islam.[2] In the long run, these possibilities were more fully realized for the *adab* culture than the scientific. Nonetheless, change was substantial, as I shall try to illustrate primarily by discussing efforts of the Istanbul and Cairo governments.

As of 1800, the world of knowledge displayed important problems inherited from preceding periods. In the domain of religious studies, recent scholarship makes us aware of creativity in this period, yet does not change the impression that this was not a great age of Islamic scholarship.[3] As for mysticism, the most pervasive problem of the world of knowledge was that this most popular form of religious expression was largely dominated not by the *sharia*-mindedness of orders like the Naqshbandiyya, but by what Gilsenan calls the mentality of the "tangled magic garden" of the ecstatics and thaumaturgics.[4] Many signs indicate that this esotericism, and not the rationalism of the *ulama*, had suffused the Islamic cultures rather generally. Not only the wisdom of the dervish sheikh, but the crafts in the bazaar, even the intellectual skills of the scribe in a government office, were regarded as secrets acquired not through a rationally ordered teaching program, but through association with an adept. The worldly literary culture, too, displayed a preference for obscure expression that harmonized with the esotericism of the mystics, even if independent in origin. Nonetheless, the worldliness of the *adibs*, at least among the Ottoman elites, had begun to take on a new dimension, thanks to the necessity of responding to the challenge of European power. In the nineteenth century, the literary-scribal elite would evolve into a vanguard of westernization, so creating a dangerous new duality between secular and Islamic cultural orientations. As for the philosophical-scientific tradition, finally, its major problem was that it had lost its vitality, almost its bare continuity.[5]

By the early twentieth century, educational and cultural reform had changed this picture substantially. To illustrate, I shall cite examples from major centers of reform, considering first traditional institutions, then modern government schools, then (briefly) schools of minorities and foreigners.

The traditional educational institutions were of three types: the Qur'anic elementary schools (*kuttab* in Arabic), the higher institutions of religious learning (*madrasa*), and a variety of non-scholastic institutions that served as centers for study or discussion – libraries, dervish meeting halls, courts and government offices, homes of intellectuals. These institutions, with the pious foundations that supported many of them, represented considerable investment in learning; yet there were problems with all of them. For example, the teaching methods of the *kuttab*, while not inferior to those of some Western European schools as of 1800, focused on memorization of the Qur'an, without prior instruction in classical Arabic. Especially in non-Arabic-speaking countries, such instruction was bound to produce many functional illiterates. Some of the most critical reflections on the *kuttab* come precisely from those who went on to become leading intellectuals.[6] For all, the main mental habit formed at the *kuttab* was rote learning. The *madrasas* directed this method of study at an encrustation of commentaries that had virtually obscured the seminal texts of Islamic learning. As for the libraries and the like, they were not organized for efficient use. The biography of the Ottoman scholar-statesman Ahmed Cevdet Paşa shows how much time he spent as a student going from one type of institution to another.[7]

Problems such as these led in time to efforts at reform of religious institutions. In Istanbul, where a state-centered protosecularism prevailed long before the beginning of westernization, results were slight until the Young Turk period. Reformers in Istanbul broached the idea of reforming the Qur'anic elementary schools in the 1840s, but never attacked this vested interest of the *ulama* until 1916. The Ottoman authorities then shifted responsibility for elementary education from the *şeyh ül-islâm* to the minister of education.[8]

In Egypt, the development of religious schools followed a different course, at least after Muhammad ʿAli, who attacked these schools and their endowments even more than his counterparts in Istanbul did. Yet he, too, was forced to rely on the *kuttab* and on al-Azhar for recruits for his new secular schools.[9] After the destruction of many of his reforms in the 1840s, the religious schools resumed something like their historic importance, especially since his successors failed to match the Istanbul government's performance in creating a system of secular schools. An important attempt to systematize and upgrade the *kuttab* occurred under the Egyptian education law of 1867.[10] After 1882, the British tried to establish government control over the *kuttabs* by providing grants to those that met certain standards. Yet most such schools remained outside the system, and its effects on education were slight. Cairo also took greater interest than Istanbul in the *madrasas*. Reform of al-Azhar began in 1872; more extensive measures followed in 1895–6. Through the mid twentieth century, however, al-Azhar remained a bastion of conservative resistance to change.[11]

On the other side of the region's cultural cleavage, the development of government schools proceeded with the foundation of, first, military, and then, civil institutions for elite formation. To the extent that reforms gave rise to generalized systems of modern schools, that was a by-product of reform.

In Istanbul, modern military education can be dated to the Naval Engineering Academy (1773) and the Army Engineering Academy (1793).[12] After the abolition of the Janissaries came the founding of the military medical school (1827) and Military Academy (1834) and the sending of student missions to Europe.[13] Eventually, there were also military preparatory schools, plus higher military schools in provincial centers from Baghdad to Manastir.[14]

The first institution for training civil officials was the Translation Office of the Sublime Porte, founded in 1821 to replace the Greek dragomanate. The founding of the first secular civil schools occurred in 1838–9. Other such schools followed, including the School of Civil Administration (Mülkiye Mektebi, 1859) and the Galatasaray Lycée, opened with French help in 1868.[15]

All the government schools were intended to be "higher" schools. Yet since no suitable preparatory schools existed, all had to start with preparatory instruction. Over time, a gradual upgrading occurred. For the Istanbul government, this happened when it began to extend its new schools into a generalized system. The process started with a plan of 1845, calling for a three-tiered system of reformed Qur'anic elementary schools, an intermediate level known as the *rüşdiye*, and a university (*dar ül-fünun*). None but the *rüşdiye* materialized, and they amounted only to upper primary schools. Yet by the early 1880s, there were roughly 120 *rüşdiyes* in the provinces and 20 in Istanbul. The first *rüşdiye* for girls opened in 1858.[16] The effort to create a multileveled government school system resumed with the Ottoman law of 1869 on education. This provided for a five-tiered hierarchy: a Qur'anic elementary school in every village or quarter,' a *rüşdiye* in every town of 500 households, a middle school (*idadiye*) in every town of 1,000 households, a lycée (*sultaniye*) in every province capital, and higher schools including teachers' colleges for men and women and, again, a university. There was no other legislation of such scope until 1924.[17]

Implementation of the 1869 plan was slow but perceptible. By 1918 there were eleven Ottoman lycées, of which perhaps only one was for girls. There were many *rüşdiyes*, and training colleges for men and women *rüşdiye* teachers had opened in 1848 and 1870. After several attempts, the Istanbul University (*dar ül-fünun*) finally opened in 1900.[18] Overall measures of the growth of the Ottoman school system are difficult to come by. Tibawi concludes that geographical Syria and Iraq ultimately had 570 Ottoman government schools, with 28,400 pupils in elementary and 2,100 in secondary grades, from which many had also gone on to the higher Istanbul schools.[19] Particularly when compared to the Japanese record from this period, Ottoman accomplishments were modest.

In Egypt, which led the way in reform during much of Muhammad ʿAli's reign, parallels with the sequence of events just discussed were strong. Here, too, reform began with an effort to train military elites. The first student mission to Europe departed as early as 1809. In the 1820s, a number of higher military schools were created, including a military medical school (1827). Efforts at civil elite formation began with the School of Civil Administration (Darskhâna al-Mulkiyyah, 1829) and the School of Languages (Madrasat al-Alsun, 1836).[20]

In the nineteenth century, the most important difference between Cairo and Istanbul lay in continuity of leadership. The more highly institutionalized government in Istanbul was better able to maintain policy continuity, whereas in Egypt, Muhammad ʿAli had to dismantle many of his own schools in the 1840s. After him, ʿAbbas, Saʿid, and Ismaʿil were men of varied priorities. Still, parallels between Cairo and Istanbul continued, as in the case of the Egyptian education law of 1867, Egypt's counterpart to the Ottoman law of 1869 – although Egypt's general school system still had to be based on the *kuttab*, for want of lower secular schools like the Ottoman *rüşdiye*. As in Istanbul, an important component of the effort to create a modern school system was the establishment of a normal school: the Dâr al-ʿUlûm (1872), which trained former al-Azhar students to teach in the new schools.[21]

Such parallelisms mostly ceased, however, after the British occupation in 1882. Cromer aimed to make the elementary education of the *kuttab* available to as many of the populace as possible, but he restricted government schools to producing personnel for subordinate administrative positions. To limit enrollment in government schools to what the administration could absorb, he also imposed tuition charges. There was no Egyptian university until 1908, when one was founded by private subscription. One of the saddest commentaries on Egyptian educational achievement prior to 1882 is that the British, with their limited objectives, appear to have enlarged the numbers of schools and students, though the numbers remained pitifully small. Enrollments in government primary schools rose from roughly 5,800 in 1890 to 8,600 in 1910, while secondary enrollments rose from about 700 to 2,200 over the same period.[22]

In the interwar period of nominal Egyptian independence under continued British dominance, education continued to suffer from problems that the governments of the period, with their characteristic lack of social policies, could not solve. Not only did the duality of religious and governmental institutions persist, but the governmental schools were divided at the lowest level between a category of free but terminal elementary schools, and other primary schools that charged fees and alone led on to higher levels. Through World War II, no more than a third of school-age children were in school, two-thirds of them male. There was no government-run university until 1925, when what is now Cairo University was created.[23]

In general, British rule in Egypt compounded or created a range of problems that also characterized the mandated territories of Southwest Asia, the main difference lying in the cultural content of the French and British systems. The problems included limited goals, extreme administrative centralization, examination systems designed to produce high failure rates, unabashed vocationalism of systems that equated diplomas with eligibility for government employment, emphasis on rote learning, urban bias in the availability of educational opportunities, and strong sexual inequalities.[24]

What, meantime, had the educational activities of non-Muslim minorities and foreign missionaries added to the picture? For the sake of brevity, I shall omit specifics, and say only a few words about the results that these systems achieved. In major centers, including Istanbul, Cairo, and Lebanon in general, the schools of at least some minority communities were better – sometimes also larger – than those of the local governments. Missionary schools also made pioneering contributions, especially in education for girls and in teaching scientific and technical subjects. Protestant missionaries introduced medical instruction at the Syrian Protestant College in Beirut in the 1860s and engineering at Robert College in 1912; Catholics introduced engineering at the Université Saint-Joseph in 1913.[25]

As European domination waned, how did the state of knowledge change? Literacy had grown considerably, though still within modest limits. From an overall regional rate of perhaps 1% to 2% in 1800, with wide variations by place, sex, religion, and other factors, the average literacy rate by 1914 had probably risen to 5% or 10%.

The highest rates for any zone of the Ottoman Middle East were reported for Lebanon, with about 50% literacy at that time, while the rate for the rest of Syria then stood at about 25%.[26]

These gains reflected not only educational reform, but also a media revolution. Whilst non-Muslims had printing presses much earlier, it was only in the nineteenth century that the Gutenberg age, bringing with it the cultural baggage of nineteenth-century Europe, arrived for Muslims. The history of Ottoman printing became continuous from 1783 on. The first Arabic press under Muslim control appears to be (was?) the one opened at Bulaq in 1822. Now, too, began movements of translation and later Western-inspired literary innovation, which assumed massive proportions in both Turkish and Arabic. Styles and media of communication also changed, especially with the advent of journalism and the need to appeal to a broad audience.

Together with the cultural bifurcation of the era, these changes had profound impact on the Islamic learned culture. In the realm of religious studies, a major differentiation appeared between the Turkish and Arabic parts of the Ottoman world, in the sense that Turkish ideas of reform became fixated increasingly on the state, while reformist thought in the Arab world remained largely Islamic in orientation. Islamicist intellectuals continued to emerge in Istanbul, but even more prominent were the *medrese* graduates – Keçecizade Fuad Paşa, Ahmed Cevdet Paşa – who shifted into the civil service. In contrast, Cairo became the center for a major series of Islamicist thinkers, especially from Jamal al-Din al Afghani on. In their efforts to formulate an Islamic response to the Western challenge lurked the danger that a lapse of rigor concerning the Islamic component would lead to permissive westernization. In fact, some students of al-Afghani and ʿAbduh became leading secularists. Yet the idea of returning to the fundamentals of Islam to seek a response to the demands of the modern world persisted, and the progression from the expediency of al-Afghani to the rigor of Rashid Rida points toward the Islamic resurgence of the twentieth century.[27]

As for mysticism, the situation in different parts of the Ottoman world was more uniform, for the "magic garden" mentality came under attack everywhere – from westernizers, from Muslim revivalists, and also from *sharia*-oriented Sufi orders. By the early twentieth century, the stage was set for Sufism to lose its centuries-old standing as the prevalent Muslim piety-style.

The worldly *adab* culture, in contrast, gained most in importance

under the constellation of European dominance. I have already
noted how growing interaction with the West meant the addition of
a new dimension to the old worldliness. During the nineteenth
century, the westernizing intelligentsia acquired unprecedented importance in government, especially in Istanbul. The growth of
journalism and a reading public made possible the emergence, too,
of professional *littérateurs* independent of government service and
patronage. Thanks to the prominence of nineteenth-century liber-
alism among the imported ideas, the expanded *adab* culture became
a major vehicle for articulation of protest against rapid change. The
result was ideological movements expressing their views in new-
minted terms of patriotism and liberty. The parade of movements
began with the Young Ottomans of the 1860s and 1870s and the
Young Turks of 1889 and later. Arab nationalist movements of the
interwar period, like the Egyptian Wafd, are essentially of the same
kind.[28]

The changes that occurred in the philosophical-scientific (*falsafa*)
component of the learned culture were less impressive. The virtual
collapse of the Islamic scientific tradition was one part of the problem. Beyond that, while officials and belletrists who learned French
could acquire general mastery of Western concepts with relative
facility, would-be scientists and engineers found their progress
more painful. Both Muhammad ʿAli and the Istanbul government
made progress in introducing European medicine and applied technologies in the early nineteenth century, always in support of military reform. These efforts set a persistent theme: the view of
advanced technologies as things to be bought and imported rather
than as matters of process, requiring a spirit of experimentation,
high levels of resources, and a complex network of support facilities. By the 1840s, European efforts to introduce free trade had
thwarted the spread of the new technologies, and many other
economic initiatives as well. The Egyptian case makes clear that the
decline of manufactures was also a decline in technology. Thereafter, Ottomans made some progress in fields like telegraphy,
military science, agriculture, veterinary science, and medicine.
But as long as European dominance remained strong, the conditions for a better performance than that of the early nineteenth
century did not exist.[29] For the scientific and technical culture,
unlike the literary, the similarity between the nineteenth- and the
ninth-century translation movements did not carry forward into
their results.

Educational and scientific consequences
of independence and mass mobilization

Formal independence meant a new constellation of social and political conditions, which solved some problems while creating new ones. The new order emphasized mass mobilization and social justice. Unprecedented population growth magnified the impact of these demands enormously. The result was educational achievements defined more in terms of numbers than quality. At last, Middle Eastern societies would move beyond "modernizing" their cultural elitism. Otherwise, their gains would be less impressive.

The new period began in Turkey during the Atatürk years. The first major step, in 1924, was one that most other Islamic countries would never take, namely, the unification of instruction in a secular system. Turkey's medreses were closed. Religious instruction was eliminated from urban, though not from rural, schools in 1920. Secularist and nationalist goals also led to the language reform and the shift to the Latin alphabet. While the latter step is normally justified on the ground that the Arabic alphabet was an obstacle to literacy – in fact, the Arabic alphabet does not work well for Turkish – the argument remains questionable in a comparative perspective. The Japanese, with an even less efficient writing system, have long had almost total literacy.

No one seems to have considered this point as the government pushed ahead with its populist-nationalist agenda. By 1927, the economic impossibility of creating separate schools for girls led to coeducation at all levels. Experiments with adult mass education began in the same decade. In the 1930s, a more extensive system for mass education and mobilization came into being with the people's houses (*halkevleri*) and people's rooms (*halk odaları*). A further step was the creation in 1937 of the Village Institute Program, under which young men who had served as noncommissioned officers were trained as rural teachers and sent to villages without schools, a major step in making education accessible to all. In the same decade, the Istanbul Dar ül-fünun underwent reform, emerging as Istanbul University, and the University of Ankara was created. Turkish higher education benefited from a major windfall in the many European scholars who accepted positions to escape the Nazis, although the effect of their employment was to reinforce imitation of Germanic models. The Turkish History Society and Language Society (Türk Tarih Kurumu, Dil Kurumu) played major roles in the development of scholarship and in the official effort to "purify" the language. By 1940, the 1927 literacy rate had doubled to 22% (35% for males, 10% for females).[30]

After World War II, Turkish education developed roughly in parallel with that of the Arab countries, except for the duality of secular and religious institutions that continues in the latter. Some Atatürk reforms were abandoned: the village institutes were closed, and religious education was reintroduced. Yet enrollments grew, especially at the upper levels. The number of university students more than doubled, to 65,297, between 1950 and 1960.[31]

Turkey's educational emphasis has since remained largely quantitative. A plan of the 1960s aimed to universalize primary enrollment by 1972, which would have meant doubling such enrollment over a period of fifteen years.[32] Even more dramatic was the increase in number of universities, which reached 7 in the 1960s, and 27 after the military takeover of 1980.[33]

In the Arab world, while independence has enlarged the number of states, a summary discussion may again focus on Egypt. Not only is it the largest Arab country, but many Arab countries have also standardized their educational systems along Egyptian lines, with a six-year elementary school, three-year preparatory school, three-year secondary school, and then the university.[34] In Egypt, this system assumed full form under the Nasser government, which ended the old practice of permitting only graduates of urban primary schools to continue their education and abolished fees for all levels of instruction. With such measures, enrollment rates for school-age children rose to the range from 62% in Tunisia to 90% in Jordan. Because of Egypt's extraordinary population growth, however, the absolute number of illiterates increased there, even while the enrollment rate went up, reaching 67% in 1976.[35]

Meanwhile, the numbers of students at higher levels increased disproportionately, except in vocational and technical schools. Between 1952 and 1977, enrollments in Egyptian primary schools increased 15%, while those in secondary schools gained 161% and those in universities grew by 180%. In Egypt, the abolition of fees and the opening of the universities to all who passed the General Secondary Exam increased the demand for higher education to a point that could be met only by increasing the number of universities from 4 in 1951 to 12 in 1975, not to speak of various higher institutes, or the system of external study (*intisab*), which permits anyone who cannot register as a regular student to take the same examinations and receive the same degrees, but not attend classes. By 1976–7, university enrollments had reached 454,000 for a population of 39 million.[36]

Such systems have obviously produced gains in terms of democratization. While one could dismiss these out of preference for qualitative achievements, it is important to bear in mind that the social justice Nasser identified with democracy may have required a phase of educational development oriented toward numerical expansion, even at the cost of qualitative improvement. Certainly, basic mass education has improved over much of the Middle East. Statistics of roughly 1975–80 show adult literacy rates as low as 20% to 40% in only a few places, mostly in the Arabian peninsula, Egypt at about 44% (up from 26% in 1960), and most other Arab countries at 50% to 70%. The 1979–80 rates for Iran and Turkey were 50% and 60%, respectively.[37]

Still, the populist educational policy had serious shortcomings, many of them old and endemic to the entire region. For example, despite the marked advance of women (especially from high-status families) into public and professional life, the percentages of males enrolled far exceeded those for females: 76% to 63% in Egypt in 1980, 78% to 56% in Turkey, 95% to 55% in Iraq.[38] Demand for education totally outstripped the available stock of school buildings, equipment, textbooks, and instructional staff, the result being high failure and dropout rates. These systemic inadequacies acquired new dimensions at the higher levels, thanks to lack of coordination between the expansion of enrollments and human resource needs. The consequences of Egypt's elimination of educational fees in 1962 and the opening of the bureaucracy as employer of last resort for university graduates in 1964 have been virtual collapse of educational standards and bureaucratic encephalitis. Meanwhile, the urban bias of education has generally perpetuated the neglect of rural education. Middle Eastern countries have sought to control the flood of students into the universities by requiring examinations, but the requirement has reinforced urban bias, because students from more affluent urban families prove best prepared. The competition has also produced abuses, at least in Egypt, in the form of private tutorials that have become a lucrative source of income for professors in prestige faculties. Competition for degrees and disdain for manual labor have led almost everywhere to neglect of vocational, agricultural, and technical education, thereby inhibiting development of the technical supports needed for science and medicine. In the universities, approaches to learning continue to rely heavily on memorization, and facilities are seldom available to permit adequate experimentation by students. Language of instruction remains a controversial issue in many places. Finally, the usual subordination of educational institutions to the national ministry of education, and the ministry's vulnerability to political pressures, diminish institutional flexibility.[39]

What can be said in the midst of such problems about the general development of knowledge? In the quintessentially Islamic domains of knowledge, I have already noted the paradox that the earliest leaders of the independent regimes were mostly determined secularizers. In general, the exponents of Islamic religious learning and mysticism seemed in this phase to be fighting a rearguard action.[40] Of the domains of knowledge affected by the nineteenth-century translation movements, the worldly literary culture, heir to the *adab* tradition, now continued largely in Western-derived media and genres. In science and technology – the most important successors of the *falsafa* tradition – the populist emphasis compounded pre-existing problems.

For the scientific and technical fields, the result was to set an agenda of needs and problems that has remained current into the phase of Islamic resurgence. Obviously, rapid expansion of higher education had negative effects on the capacity of the universities to support research or equip students for it. The result was over-emphasis on theory, a tendency encouraged by some of the European models followed in educational reform. Consequences of the inadequacies of the universities and of the research environment in general included the brain drain, normally to the West through the early 1970s, or the wastage of talent. While few Middle Eastern countries had long been in position to formulate a science policy – Egypt was the pioneer in the Arab world, with its national research council founded in 1939[41] – the trend was ultimately, as in education, toward centralization, which tends to subordinate scientific and technological policy-making to political forces. Partly for this reason, a common tendency in this phase was toward grand but often ill-studied projects like the Aswan Dam, and away from mundane issues like public health or solar energy. Another recurrent theme recalled the days of Muhammad ʿAli – the reliance on turnkey projects, imported machines or foreign-built plants that supposedly had only to be bought and placed in operation. Such projects made technology a primary means for assertion of Western influence in the Middle East after the end of overt colonization.[42]

Knowledge, education, and the Islamic resurgence

Since about 1973, conditions have emerged that point toward a new phase in the history of knowledge and education in the Islamic world. One part of the change was the OPEC oil price revolution and the sudden flow of wealth into some Middle Eastern countries. Another was the resurgence of Islamic consciousness and self-confidence. For the Islamic world in general, these two facts are simply the most conspicuous data in a complex set of changes following from the breakup of the old Western ascendancy. It is too early to write the history of education under this new constellation, although many changes could be catalogued. What is clearer is how Muslim activists view the meaning of the resurgence for knowledge and education.

The most basic point that requires notice is a shift of mood. Instead of the once central question of how Islam could respond to Western-defined challenges of "modernity," the recent literature on Islam and development asserts control of the agenda, asking instead how Muslims can absorb what they want of the conveniences of the outside world into a social order where it is assumed that Islamic values will reign as the organizing principles. For education, the answers include proposals to end institutional dualism through a reintegration into unitary educational systems designed to prepare their students for life in a *sharia*-based community. Such a reintegration means a massive effort, not only to reorganize institutions or prepare new textbooks, but to rethink the very organization of knowledge. This effort would have important implications for many fields. For literature and the arts, it would mean bringing the muse under Islamic discipline. For the social and natural sciences it would mean an end to ideas of science for its own sake. Islamic science must differ from Western science in the philosophy or ideology that forms its context, or even in its fundamental assumptions. Finally, for partisans of this point of view, controversies over languages of instruction and publication must be resolved in favor of Islamic languages, especially Arabic.[43] Above all, advocates of the Islamic resurgence demand a new synthesis of all fields of endeavour under a *sharia*-oriented religious consciousness. The clearest indications of this demand are the new values attached to the Islamic concept of *tawhid* – for example, political unity in support of the revolution in Iran; or unity of humankind, of humankind and nature, of knowledge and values in a proposed model of Islamic science.[44]

As concerns the implications of this demand for specific fields of knowledge, science and technology receive particular attention. True, not everything that has happened under the "sign" of Islamic resurgence is properly attributable to it. The improvement of scientific facilities is largely an oil-related matter of economics. Improvements in the size and quality of scientific communities have roots in the preceding phases, too. Perhaps most important, it would be a gross exaggeration to assume that all scientists from Islamic countries are partisans of the resurgence. A recent survey of their points of view found a range from the belief that science is value-free, to the view that Islamic science should be based on entirely different assumptions from Western science. Yet, if partly because prior levels of output were low by international standards, recent events do indicate an important growth of scientific achievement in Islamic countries.[45] Since this is a kind of "Islamic resurgence" in science and technology, it is appropriate to comment on it and consider how well it is likely to answer the expectations of the pious activists.

A paradox of the OPEC era is that the increase in spending on science and technology has perpetuated technological dependence and reliance on turnkey projects.[46] Still, the new Islamic consciousness has meant greater interest in local problems, and thus a shift toward practical applications. Organizations for scientific policy-making have undergone reorganization from North Africa to Pakistan. As was the case earlier in Turkey, experiments in new models of university organization have occurred in Pakistan, Saudi Arabia, Kuwait, and Algeria – for example, by combining faculties of science, engineering, and medicine with those for Islamic studies. To support the effort at Arabization, the Arab League Educational, Cultural and Scientific Organization (ALECSO) created a permanent bureau for Arabization as early as 1967, and it has since published more than 50 trilingual technical glossaries. Efforts at Islamization of science have progressed through study of the history of Islamic science (a field that long predates the Islamic resurgence) and of Muslim scientists' views about science, attempts to develop a model of Islamic science, identification of many fields of Western science that are compatible with Islamic values, and efforts, especially by the Hamdard National Foundation in Pakistan, to redevelop Islamic medicine.[47]

An important facet of the recent development of science lies in growth of support facilities. Here may be noted the continued importance of foreign technical assistance and the growth of national centers for documentation. Another important step was the formation of regional entities for coordinating scientific policy and projects. Such was the alliance for Regional Cooperation and Development among Turkey, Iran, and Pakistan, which Iran dissolved in 1981, and more recently ALECSO, among other organizations in the Arab world.[48]

New developments in the brain drain, while depriving some countries (like the Sudan) of qualified personnel, have also supported scientific development in some ways. The economics of the OPEC era reduced migration to Europe and America, but created new possibilities for movement among Islamic countries. The numbers migrating within the region probably exceed those that previously went to the West. For some countries, the earlier brain drain to the West has also begun to yield payoffs. In Turkey and Pakistan, this has happened through programs designed to bring expatriates back as consultants. Pakistani expatriates have organized such efforts spontaneously and have, for good or ill, played a major role in that country's nuclear program. Pakistan's eminent expatriate, Nobel laureate Abdus Salam, has made an exceptional contribution in calling for international centers of excellence for specific fields in the Middle East. In addition to several already created, he has advocated others for problems – irrigation, schistosomiasis, marine pollution – that need the joint efforts of the scientists of the region.[49]

How likely are current developments in fields like medicine, agriculture, pollution control, nuclear energy, solar energy, microelectronics, and communications, including satellite communications, to conform to strict Islamic expectations? In this regard, a key issue will be whether *sharia*-minded activists of today can channel scientific development any better than their predecessors of bygone centuries maintained the *sharia*-conformity of the *falasifa* of their time. *Falsafa* was even then regarded as the most alien branch of knowledge from the Islamic point of view.[50] Today, Islamic science is no doubt possible if we mean by that the application, by Muslims, according to Islamic priorities, of techniques and ideas drawn from what used to be called Western, and can now better be called international, science. Even here, as in ʿAbduh's attempt to reconcile faith and reason, there lurks the danger of a permissive reconciliation, in which the Islamic component may be submerged. To demand more than this kind of Islamic science – for example, creation of science that differs in kind – is like demanding reinvention of the wheel.[51]

The Middle Eastern experience in comparative perspective

To evaluate the Middle Eastern experience more fully, it helps to look at it comparatively. For this purpose, the most appropriate comparisons are with the South and East Asian centers of civilization.

Ordering the comparisons from least to most successful in terms
of modern development of education and science, I begin with
China. In view of the country's great intellectual tradition and many
important technical discoveries, this low ranking may seem un-
warranted. Yet China has several qualities that justify the ranking
and also resemble traits of the Islamic world. Such traits include
China's traditionally self-centered worldview and faith in the superiority of its own civilization, a faith fully justified until the
nineteenth century. These facts, coupled with China's huge population and the consistency across space and time of its dominant
culture, are enough to explain its resistance to alien ideas. But what
explains the fact that China's technical discoveries did not launch an
industrial revolution, or make modern science China's gift to the
world? In the work of Joseph Needham, the greatest Western
historian of Chinese science, this problem remains unsolved. For a
recent Chinese commentator, however, the answer is obvious,
namely, that China's dominant institutions and Confucian ideology
emphasized harmony, organicism, synthesis – exactly the opposites
of the analytical, open-ended approach essential to science. For this
Chinese commentator, it is no accident that modern science developed in the European environment, characterized not by a single
monolithic state and dominant philosophy, but by pluralism of
political and other authorities.[52] The argument is one that architects
of the Islamic resurgence might well consider. In recent years,
where the People's Republic has been most successful is not in
qualitative terms, especially under the conditions of Mao's permanent revolution, but in democratization of opportunity. China's
historically high literacy rates, 15% to 25% already in the early
nineteenth century, stood at an estimated 69% in 1982, an impressive advance for a nation of a billion.[53]

China's success in improving conditions for its populace also
contrasts remarkably with the Indian record. India in the 1980s is
home at once to half the world's illiterates and to the world's third
largest scientific community, which has produced such varied
achievements as a nuclear explosion in 1974 and a communications
satellite launching in an Indian-made vehicle in 1980.[54] The roots of
India's pardoxical record lie partly in Hindu tradition and partly in
the British impact. Hindu tradition has been important both in its
lack of the closedness or exclusivism of either Islamic or Confucian
thought – the result being fewer barriers to intercultural borrowings
– and in the tolerance of inequality rooted in the caste system.
British rule has contributed to India's performance precisely be-

cause it was longer and more sustained than the imperialist impact on any other major Asian civilizational center. Although the British impact at first deindustrialized India as it did the Middle East, the British ultimately left infrastructural improvements in the form of railroads and communications, rudimentary science-based public services in fields like geology and surveying, and a university system – not to mention educational institutions that Indians founded in reaction to British innovations. Even the survival of English as national lingua franca proved important for science by assuring access, despite resentments, to international scholarship. The result is a nation of over 700 million, which – with a literacy rate of only 36% in 1982 – nonetheless had 119 universities plus hundreds of other institutions of higher learning, which added about 150,000 each year to its scientific community of 2.5 million, and which had 130 specialized research laboratories under government agencies and 600 research laboratories in public and private companies. Prime Minister Nehru (1947–64) set the example for government patronage of science and technology.[55] How unfortunate for poor Indians that this patronage did not include the egalitarianism of the Middle East or China.

To account for Japan's extraordinary achievements, finally, is a much greater challenge. Here I can only cite factors that stand out most in comparison with the Middle East. The first point is that despite having the world's least efficient writing system, Japan enjoyed literacy rates of perhaps 25% to 40% already in the early nineteenth century and virtually 100% today.[56] As Charles Issawi and others have emphasized, Japan's one great resource is, in fact, its population.[57] Entering its modern era with a literacy rate approaching that of Egypt today, the country simply never experienced such hard choices between qualitative and quantitative educational goals as we have noted elsewhere in Asia.

Prior to its "opening" in 1853–4, Japan had a long history of cultural borrowing and a pluralism of political and other authorities that more resembled European than other Asian societies. Compared to China, the country was small and accessible all round by sea, lacking the mass and inertia that enabled most Chinese to ignore the Western impact as long as they did. With Japan's "opening," the Tokugawa order quickly collapsed amid revolutionary change in both polity and society – a combination that no Middle Eastern country experienced to comparable extent until the Turkish republic. Thereafter, partly by limiting its development projects to what it could finance with domestic capital, Japan escaped the

Middle East's slide into bankruptcy, industrialized rapidly, and by the turn of the century had begun to command formal European recognition of its great power status.

By the 1890s, Japan had become the first Asian nation to create a Western-style national secular school system, from compulsory elementary schools through university. By 1900, there were two national universities and several institutions of higher learning founded on private initiative. Some features of university development in this period are noteworthy in comparison with later Middle-Eastern experience. The question of the language for scientific instruction had already been settled – in favor of Japanese. Already, there was experimentation with different European models of university organization. The idea of "science for its own sake" was not accepted at first. Facilities for research, institutional autonomy, and academic freedom were initially scarce to nonexistent. There was a tendency to see science and technology as a continuum, all foreign-derived and most important in its practical applications, in which Japan needed constantly to catch up. Japanese social traditions also exerted a lingering influence. Much of the early scientific community were of samurai origins, scholarship, like the martial arts, having been an acceptable pursuit for samurai under the old order. As a result, the professoriate was characterized by such seeming irregularities as inheritance of professorships by sons-in-law of the previous incumbents. Closer inspection shows, however, that academic performance determined a young man's eligibility to marry a professor's daughter. Many of these traits changed after 1900,[58] but they do suggest that Middle Eastern higher education might have fared better if the gap between decline of the old *madrasas* or the *falsafa* tradition and the rise of the modern universities had not been so great. Japan certainly illustrated that exact fidelity to Western models is not the only way.

What is most impressive in the Japanese case is the breadth of governmental, societal, and business-sector support for education and science, and the speed of development. Japanese universities quickly began to achieve world "firsts" – the first professional society for seismology (1880), the first chair in genetics (1917). Much of this would not have been possible without rapid industrialization, which benefited from a close relationship between government and business, anticipating that institutionalized since World War II in the Ministry of International Trade and Industry. Already by the World War I period, private initiative was a leading factor in the establishment of such important facilities as the Research Institute for Physics and Chemistry.[59] Thereafter, education, technology, and industry seemed to advance together, resuming their progress after World War II.

Can the Middle East use the resources of the OPEC era to consolidate its recent populist gains while also laying the bases for qualitatively more significant achievements, especially in science and technology? Can it overcome cultural dualism in a way compatible with both the current Islamic awareness and the advance of science? Can the Middle East achieve the broad development required to support these efforts? In comparative Asian perspective, these are probably the greatest questions before the region today.

NOTES

1 Marshall G. S. Hodgson, *The Venture of Islam: Conscience and History in a World Civilization* (3 vols.; Chicago: University of Chicago Press, 1974), I, 238–9 and passim; cf. Gustave von Grunebaum, *Islam: Essays in the Nature and Growth of a Cultural Tradition* (2nd ed.; London: Routledge & Kegan Paul, 1961), pp. 111–26. I owe thanks to several colleagues at Ohio State University for their assistance: Alan Beyerchen, James Bartholomew, Dona Straley, and Michael Zwettler.

2 Ibrahim Abu-Lughod, *Arab Rediscovery of Europe: A Study in Cultural Encounters* (Princeton: Princeton University Press, 1963), pp. 58–9.

3 Gilbert Delanoue, *Moralistes et politiques musulmans dans l'Egypte du XIXe siècle (1798–1882)* (2 vols.; Cairo: Institut Français d'Archéologie Orientale du Caire, 1982), II, 560; Peter Gran, *Islamic Roots of Capitalism: Egypt, 1760–1840* (Austin: University of Texas Press, 1979).

4 Michael Gilsenan, *Saint and Sufi in Modern Egypt: An Essay in the Sociology of Religion* (Oxford: Clarendon Press, 1973).

5 Niyazi Berkes, *The Development of Secularism in Turkey* (Montreal: McGill University Press, 1964); Abdülhak Adnan Adıvar, *Osmanlı Türkelerinde Ilim* (Istanbul: Remzi Kitabevi, 1943), passim; Aydın Sayılı, "The Place of Science in the Turkish Movement of Westernization, and Atatürk," *Erdem*, 1 (1985), 25–81; Delanoue, *Moralistes*, I, 6, 17–18, 144–5; II, 350 and passim; Fazlur Rahman, *Islam and Modernity: Transformation of an Intellectual Tradition* (Chicago: University of Chicago Press, 1982), pp. 33–9, 46–7, 70–2.

6 Taha Husayn, *Al-Ayyam* (3 vols.; Cairo, 1981–2), I, 28ff.; idem, *An Egyptian Childhood*, trans. E. H. Paxton (London: G. Routledge, 1932), pp. 27ff.; Osman Ergin, *Istanbul Mektepleri ve Ilim, Terbiye ve San' at Müesseseleri Dolayısile Türkiye Maarif Tarihi* (5 vols.; Istanbul, 1939–43), I, 70, n. 2; II, 384–6.

7 Richard L. Chambers, "The Education of a Nineteenth-Century Ottoman Âlim, Ahmed Cevdet Paşa," *International Journal of Middle East Studies*, 4 (1973), 440–64.

8 Ergin, *Türkiye Maarif Tarihi*, I, 102–20, 135–42; II, 387–97, 481–486; III,

725–35; Abdul Latif Tibawi, *Islamic Education: Its Traditions and Modernization into the Arab National Systems* (London: Luzac, 1972); pp. 65–7, 82–3; Niyazi Berkes, *The Development of Secularism in Turkey* (Montreal: McGill University Press, 1964), pp. 400–16.

9 J. Heyworth-Dunne, *An Introduction to the History of Education in Modern Egypt* (London: Luzac & Co., 1939), pp. 154–7, 210–17; Ahmad ʿIzzat ʿAbd al-Karim, *Ta'rikh al-Taʿlimfi ʿAsrMuhammad ʿAli* (Cairo, 1938), pp. 555–93.

10 Heyworth-Dunne, *Introduction*, pp. 358–74; Delanoue, *Moralistes*, ii, 507–12.

11 Robert L. Tignor, *Modernization and British Colonial Rule in Egypt, 1882–1914* (Princeton, N.J.: Princeton University Press, 1966), pp. 329–30; Rahman, *Islam and Modernity*, pp. 63–9; Bayard Dodge, *Al-Azhar: A Millennium of Muslim Learning* (Washington: Middle East Institute, 1974), pp. 111–44; Egyptian Ministry of Awqaf, *Ta'rikh al-Azhar wa Tatawwurihi* (Cairo, 1964) (not seen); Joseph S. Szyliowicz, *Education and Modernization in the Middle East* (Ithaca: Cornell University Press, 1973), pp. 191–3.

12 Ergin, *Türkiye Maarif Tarihi*, ii, 264–80.

13 Ibid., ii, 280–325, 356–67.

14 Ibid., ii, 418–23; iii, 712, 716–24, 742–3.

15 Ibid., ii, 400–5, 495–517.

16 Ibid., ii, 355, 367–75, 381–3; iii, 738.

17 Andreas M. Kazamias, *Education and the Quest for Modernity in Turkey* (London: George Allen & Unwin, 1966).

18 Ergin, *Türkiye Maarif Tarihi*, ii, 465–8, 475–89, 557–72; iii, 709–10, 997–1041; iv, 1188–93.

19 Abdul Latif Tibawi, *A Modern History of Syria, Including Lebanon and Palestine* (London: Macmillan, 1969), pp. 168–9, 181–2, 194–6; idem, *Islamic Education*, pp. 64, 82–4.

20 Heyworth-Dunne, *Education in Egypt*, pp. 104–5, 117–210; Ahmad ʿIzzat ʿAbd al-Karim, *Ta'rikh al-Taʿlim*, pp. 251–422.

21 Heyworth-Dunne, *Introduction*, pp. 288 ff.; Delanoue, *Moralistes*, ii, 512–14.

22 Tignor, *Modernization*, pp. 323–9; Szyliowicz, *Education and Modernization*, pp. 122–34; Saʿid Ismaʿil ʿAli, *Qadaya al-Taʿlimfi ʿAhd al-Ihtilal* (Cairo, 1974), pp. 127–216; Muhammad ʿAbduh, *Al-Aʿmal al-Kamila*, ed. Muhammad ʿUmara, Vol. iii (Beirut, 1972), pp. 105–20.

23 Szyliowicz, *Education and Modernization*, pp. 180–96.

24 Joseph Szyliowicz, unpublished paper on knowledge and education in the twentieth century (cited below as Szyliowicz, "Knowledge and Education"), prepared for Princeton working group on modernization of the Ottoman Empire and successor states (a collective volume on this theme is in preparation, ed. L. Carl Brown); Edith A. S. Hanania,

"Access of Arab Women to Higher Education," in *Arab Women and Education* (Beirut: Institute for Women's Studies in the Arab World, 1980), p. 35. Works on specific countries in this period include: ʿAli, *Qadaya al-Taʿlim*; Abdul Latif Tibawi, *Arab Education in Mandatory Palestine: A Study of Three Decades of British Administration* (London: Luzac, 1956); Navil Ayyub Badran, *Al-Taʿlim waʾl Tahdith fiʾl-Mujtamaʿ al-ʿArabi al-Filastini*, Vol. I: *ʿAhd al-Intidab* (Beirut, 1969).

25 I plan to survey minority and foreign schools more fully in my essay on knowledge and education in the nineteenth century, prepared for the Princeton working group on modernization of the Ottoman Empire and successor states; among the relevant sources, see K. S. Salibi, *The Modern History of Lebanon* (London and New York: Weidenfeld & Nicolson, 1965), pp. 123–6, 130–3; Abdul Latif Tibawi, *Arabic and Islamic Themes: Historical, Educational, and Literary Studies* (London: Luzac, 1976), pp. 253–85; Heyworth-Dunne, *Introduction*, pp. 217–84, 308–12, 330–41, 406–24, 436–7.

26 Charles Issawi, *An Economic History of the Middle East and North Africa* (New York: Columbia University Press, 1982), p. 114 (7% literate in Egypt, 1907; about 25% in Syria); Stanford J. Shaw and Ezel Kural Shaw, *History of the Ottoman Empire and Modern Turkey*, Vol. II: *Reform, Revolution, and Republic: The Rise of Modern Turkey, 1808–1975* (Cambridge and New York: Cambridge University Press, 1977), p. 387 (barely above 10% literate in Turkey in 1927).

27 Albert Hourani, *Arabic Thought in the Liberal Age, 1789–1929* (Oxford: Oxford University Press, 1962), pp. 160ff.; Malcolm H. Kerr, *Islamic Reform: The Political and Legal Theories of Muhammad ʿAbduh and Rashid Rida* (Berkeley & Los Angeles: University of California Press, 1966), chs. 1, 7; Hamid Enayat, *Modern Islamic Political Thought* (Austin: University of Texas Press, 1982), ch. 3.

28 Şerif Mardin, *The Genesis of Young Ottoman Thought: A Study in the Modernization of Turkish Political Ideas* (Princeton, N.J.: Princeton University Press, 1962), ch. 3; Carter Vaughn Findley, "The Advent of Ideology in the Islamic Middle East," *Studia Islamica*, 56 (1982), 152–3, 162–5, 173–4, 179.

29 Charles Issawi, *An Economic History of the Middle East and North Africa*, pp. 150–9; idem, *The Economic History of Turkey, 1800–1914* (Chicago: University of Chicago Press, 1980), pp. 272–320; idem, *The Economic History of the Middle East, 1800–1914* (Chicago: University of Chicago Press, 1966), pp. 38–9, 389–402; Afaf Lutfi al-Sayyid Marsot, *Egypt in the Reign of Muhammad Ali* (Cambridge & New York: Cambridge University Press, 1984), pp. 162ff.; Antoine B. Zahlan, "Established Patterns of Technology Acquisition in the Arab World," in *Technology Transfer and Change in the Arab World*, ed. A. B. Zahlan (Oxford & New York: Pergamon Press, 1978), pp. 1–27; Meh-

met Genç, "Foreign Trade and Government Policies towards Industrialization in the Ottoman Empire, 1700–1850," paper prepared for the International Conference on "Problems and Policies of Industrialization," Istanbul, 24–8 August 1981; Edward C. Clark, "The Ottoman Industrial Revolution," *International Journal of Middle East Studies*, 5 (1974), 65–76.

30 Szyliowicz, *Education and Modernization*, pp. 199–230.

31 Ibid., pp. 330–2; Rahman, *Islam and Modernity*, pp. 92–8.

32 Szyliowicz, *Education and Modernization*, pp. 347–8.

33 Ibid., pp. 375–86.

34 Fahim I. Qubain, *Education and Science in the Arab World* (Baltimore: Johns Hopkins University Press, 1966), pp. 5–7; cf. John Waterbury, *The Egypt of Nasser and Sadat: The Political Economy of Two Regimes* (Princeton: Princeton University Press, 1983), p. 235; ʿAbd al-Ghani ʿAbbud, *Al-Aydiyulujiyya waʾl-Tarbiya* (Cairo, 1978), p. 488.

35 Szyliowicz, "Knowledge and Education"; Waterbury, *Egypt*, p. 220.

36 Qubain, *Education and Science*, p. 76; Rahman, *Islam and Modernity*, pp. 98–104; Waterbury, *Egypt*, pp. 218–21, 234–41; Szyliowicz, "Knowledge and Education"; Muhammad Munir Mursi, *Al-Taʿlim al-ʿAmm fi ʾl-Bilad al-ʿArabiyya* (Cairo, 1974), pp. 66–84; Jamil Saliba, *Mustaqbal al-Tarbiya fi ʾl-ʿAlam al-ʾArabi* (Beirut, 1967).

37 *World Tables*, Vol. II: *Social Data from the Data Files of the World Bank* (3rd ed.; Baltimore: Johns Hopkins University Press, 1983), passim.

38 Szyliowicz, "Knowledge and Education"; Clement Henry Moore, *Images of Development: Egyptian Engineers in Search of Industry* (Cambridge, Mass.: MIT Press, 1980), ch. 7.

39 Qubain, *Education and Science*, passim; Szyliowicz, "Knowledge and Education"; Moore, *Images of Development*, chs. 4–7; Mursi, *Al-Taʿlim al-ʿAmm*, pp. 9–93, 304–27.

40 Cf. Rahman, *Islam and Modernity*, pp. 84–91.

41 Qubain, *Education and Science*, pp. 264ff.; Moore, *Images of Development*, pp. 86–8; Ziauddin Sardar, *Science and Technology in the Middle East* (London & New York: Longman, 1982), p. 6.

42 Antoine B. Zahlan, *Science and Science Policy in the Arab World* (London: Croom Helm, 1980), pp. 18–20; Moore, *Images of Development*, chs. 5, 8–10.

43 Syed Sajjad Husain and Syed Ali Ashraf, *Crisis in Muslim Education* (Sevenoaks, UK: Hodder & Stoughton, 1979), passim; Ismaʾil R. al-Faruqi and Abdullah Omar Nasseef, eds., *Social and Natural Sciences: The Islamic Perspective* (Sevenoaks, UK: Hodder & Stoughton, 1981); Muhammad Munir Mursi, *Al-Tarbiya al-Islamiyya: Usuluha wa Tatawwuruha fi ʾl-Bilad al-ʿArabiyya* (Cario, 1982); ʿAbd al-Ghani ʿAbbud, *Al-Tarbiya al-Islamiyya fi ʾl-Qarn al-Khamis ʿAshar al-Hijri* (Cairo, 1982); Muhammad Fadil al-Jamali, *Nahwa Tawhid al-Fikr al-Tarbawi fi ʾl-ʿAlam al-Islami* (Tunis, 1972); Anwar al-Jundi, *Al-Tarbiya*

wa Bina² al-Ajyal fi Daw² al-Islam (Beirut, 1975); Ahmad Muhammad Jamal, *Nahwa Tarbiya Islamiyya* (Jidda, 1980).

44 Sardar, *Science and Technology*, pp. 14–23.

45 Ibid., pp. 19–20; Moore, *Images of Development*, pp. 84–6. For recent scientific publication in Arabic, see the science and technology listings in *Al-Fihrist: Quarterly Index to Arabic Periodical Literature* (Beirut, 1981–) from journals like *Al-ʿIlm wa 'l-Mujtamaʿ* (Cairo), *Al-Majalla al-ʿArabiyya li-'l-ʿUlum* (Tunis), *Majallat al-Bahth al-ʿIlmi al-ʿArabi* (Baghdad), and *Al-Naft wa- l-Tanmiya* (Baghdad), most of them launched in the 1980s.

46 Zahlan, "Established Patterns of Technology Acquisition," pp. 15–18; idem, *Science and Science Policy*, pp. 17–20.

47 Sardar, *Science and Technology*, pp. 4–23; Ziauddin Sardar, ed., *The Touch of Midas: Science, Values and Environment in Islam and the West* (Manchester: Manchester University Press, 1984).

48 Sardar, *Science and Technology*, pp. 57–71, 83–116.

49 Ibid., pp. 11–14, 140–1; Antoine B. Zahlan, ed., *The Arab Brain Drain* (London: Ithaca Press, 1981); Ismail Serageldin et al., *Manpower and International Labor Migration in the Middle East and North Africa* (New York: Oxford University Press, 1983).

50 Von Grunebaum, *Islam*, pp. 119–21.

51 Cf. Rahman, *Islam and Modernity*, pp. 130–62.

52 Wen-yuan Qian, "Science Development: Sino-Western Comparative Insights," *Knowledge: Creation, Diffusion, Utilization*, 6 (1985), 392–3, 403; idem, *The Great Inertia: Scientific Stagnation in Traditional China* (London: Croom Helm, 1985); Tong B. Tang, *Science and Technology in China* (London: Longman, 1984).

53 Evelyn Rawski, *Education and Popular Literacy in Chʾing China* (Ann Arbor: University of Michigan Press, 1979), p. 23; *World Tables*, II, 21.

54 Carol Honsa, "India: Fire and Ashes," *Christian Science Monitor*, 7 September 1982, p. 1.

55 Ward Morehouse, "Myth and Reality: Animadversions on Science, Technology, and Society in India," *Knowledge: Creation, Diffusion, Utilization*, 6 (1985), 412–14; Claude A. Alvares, *Homo Faber: Technology and Culture in India, China and the West, 1500 to the Present Day* (The Hague & Boston: M. Nijhoff, 1980); Baldev R. Nayar, *India's Quest for Technological Independence* (New Delhi: Lancers Publishers, 1983) (not seen).

56 Ronald P. Dore, *Education in Tokugawa Japan* (Berkeley & Los Angeles: University of California Press, 1965), pp. 317–22.

57 Charles Issawi, "Why Japan?" in *Arab Resources: The Transformation of a Society*, ed. Ibrahim Ibrahim (London: Croom Helm, 1983), pp. 283–300.

58 James R. Bartholomew, "Japanese Culture and the Problem of Modern Science," in *Science and Values*, ed. E. Mendelsohn and A. Thackray

(New York: Humanities Press, 1974), pp. 109–55; idem, "The 'Feudal-istic' Legacy of Japanese Science," *Knowledge: Creation, Diffusion, Utilization*, 6 (1985), 350–76; Alun M. Anderson, *Science and Technology in Japan* (London: Longman, 1984).

59 Bartholomew, "'Feudalistic' Legacy," pp. 362, 367–70.

INDEX

Fernea, Elizabeth, 97
Fertile Crescent, 120
Feudalism, 49
France, 11, 20, 33, 35, 36; water mills,
  5
French language, 6
Frederick II, 14
Free Economic Society (Russia), 16
Fundamentalist movements, 123, 127.
  See also Islamic resurgence

Geertz, Clifford, 92, 93
Gellner, Ernest, 92, 95, 107
Germany, 35, 36
al-Ghazali, 115
Goldenweister, Alexander, 93
Governments: inhibiting role of, 6, 7;
  medieval European, 11; Middle
  Eastern, 7–8; social composition of,
  6, 7–8; Western, 7
Great Britain, 5, 22, 47, 66, 133;
  colonies, 29; and Egyptian
  development, 70, 85, 136; hydraulic
  investments in Egypt, 71–4, 85;
  impact on Egypt, 135–6; impact on
  India, 146–7; multinationals, 84
Great Depression, 34, 71, 80
Great Tradition, 107
Greece, 17, 32; literacy, 18
Greek language, 9, 134
Greeks, 8, 18, 23, 24
Gross Domestic Product (GDP), 53–6
Gross National Product (GNP), 3, 62;
  Argentina, 18–19; Iraq, 53; Mexico,
  19
Guatemala, 20
Gulf states, 36, 37, 38

Halpern, Manfred, 104
Hamdard National Foundation
  (Pakistan), 144
Hanseatic League, 11
Hansen, Bent, 57, 66, 67
Harb, Tala' at, 79, 81, 84
Hebrew language, 9
Heliopolis-Oasis Company, 75
Hindu tradition, 146
Hopkins, N., 96

Ibn Khaldun, 6

Identity: cultural, 99–105 *passim*;
  national, 99, 100
Ikhwan (Syria), 125
'ilm, 130
Immigration Act of 1921, 34
Imperial Library (St. Petersburg), 16
India, 5–6, 13, 19, 21, 22, 56, 82;
  British impact on, 146–7; canals, 5;
  cotton, 82–3
Indians, 83, 147
Indonesia, 93, 97
Industrialization, 17, 23, 78, 81–5
Inheritance, in Muslim law, 116
Integration, 36, 100
International Migration (Ferenczi and
  Willcox), 29
Investments: in industry, 78; in
  infrastructure, 74–6; in inventories,
  76
Iran, 22, 23, 131, 141, 143, 144; ports,
  50; *qanats*, 6; revolution, 47;
  windmills, 5
Iranians, 18, 23, 24, 32
Iraq, 54, 56, 122, 124, 127; canals, 6;
  foreign labor, 38–9; Gross Domestic
  Product, 53, 54, 55; oil, 36–7, 46,
  47, 48; schools, 135. *See also*
  Women
'irfan, 130
Irrigation, 6, 67, 72–4
Isfahan, 17
Islam, 97, 113; and development, 143;
  philosophic-scientific tradition, 132;
  post-traditional forms, 92, 95
Islamic civilization, 130
Islamic countries, 139, 144, 145
Islamic dress. *See* Muslim dress
Islamic resurgence, 103, 124, 131, 137,
  142–6, *passim. See also*
  Fundamentalist movements
Islamic science, 143–4, 145
Islamic values, 143
Islamic world, 142–3; compared with
  China, 146
Isma'il (Egypt), 66, 135
Isma'ilis, 95
Issawi, Charles, 32, 56, 66, 100, 108,
  147
Istanbul, 9, 17, 133, 134, 136, 137,
  138
Istanbul University (Dar ul-Funun),
  134–5, 139
Italy, 17, 20, 31, 35

Modernity, 105, 107, 143; adaptive path to, 106; fruits of, 97; viewed by Rousseau, 99. *See also* Tradition

Modernization, 12, 89, 94, 100, 107; adaptive 98–9; adaptive and inverse, 92; alternative courses, 103–8; comparative literature on, 91; as disruptive process, 100–1; innovative aspects, 103; institutional vectors of, 104; policy, 97; process, 106; studies, 3; theories, 95

Moghuls (India), 6

Monetary system, 76–8, 79, 81

Monetization, 14

Mongol invasion, 4

Morocco, 32

Moscow, 15

Moscow University, 15

Mount Lebanon, 33

Muhammad Ali, 9, 21, 66, 71, 135, 138, 142

Murids, 95

Muslim activists. *See* Islamic resurgence

Muslim Brothers, 123

Muslim dress, 125, 126, 127. *See also* Veiling

Muslims, 115, 137, 145; refugees, 32; women, 120

Mysticism, 132, 137, 142

Napoleon, 14

Naqshabandiyya, 132

Nash, J., 96

Nasser regime, 72, 105, 140

Nasserism, 123

National Bank of Egypt (NBE), 77, 79, 80, 81, 84

National consciousness, 99, 101, 102

Nation-state, 100, 102, 104

Naval Engineering Academy (Istanbul), 134

Navigation Laws, 11

Nazis, 139

Needham, Joseph, 146

Nehru, Jawaharlal, 147

Newton, Isaac, 20

Nigeria, 47

Nile, 4, 6

Normans, 6

North Africa, 22, 32, 35, 106, 144

North America, 5. *See also* United States

Norway, 46

Novikov, Nikolai, 16

Oil, 23, 44, 144; boom, 3, 36; exporting countries, 49, 52–3; future prices, 48–9; impact, 37; prices, 44, 45, 51; production, 46; revenues, 47, 50, 56

Open Door policy, 124

Opium war, 21

Ordin-Nashchokin, Afanasii L., 16

Organization for Economic Cooperation and Development (OECD), 35

Organization of Petroleum Exporting Countries (OPEC), 44, 49, 144, 145, 149; aid, 62; funds, 60–1; future of, 63; pricing, 47, 143; production limitations, 46–7

Osaka, 12, 14

Ottoman Empire, 22, 32, 77, 137; army, 33; authorities, 133; education, 134–5; elites, 132; law, 134, 135; policy, 8; printing, 137; progress, 138; trade, 18

Ottomans, 8, 11, 17, 33

Pakistan, 57, 144, 145

Palestine, 32, 33

Palestinians, 33, 39

Pan-Arab labor, 105

Parsees, 82

Patrimonialism, 92

Patron-client networks, 94, 102

Persians, 24. *See also* Iranians

Peter the Great, 14, 15

Philippines, 22

Phoenicians, 24

Plantagenets, 6

Pluralism, 147; cultural, 41; sectarian, 102

Poland, 31; peasants, 30–31

The Polish Peasant in Europe and America (Thomas and Znaniecki), 29

Population growth, 4, 12–13, 69

Populism, 107

Pososhkov, Ivan T., 16

Potosi (Bolivia), 18